KALI

LINUX

Comprehensive Beginners Guide to Learn Kali Linux Step by Step

Ethan Thorpe

Table of Contents

Chapter 1

An Introduction to Kali Linux

KALI LINUX

K ali is a flavor of Linux distributions that is Debian-based and was created specifically for its application in the security domain, which focused primarily on Security Auditing and Penetration Testing. Kali comes equipped with hundreds of tools that are aimed at various tasks used for information security. These include Security Research, Penetration Testing, Reverse Engineering, Computer Forensics, etc. Offensive Security, a company that is a world leader in information security training, is the company that developed Kali Linux and now funds its maintenance.

Kali Linux is a successor of BackTrack Linux. BackTrack Linux was a Linux distribution which was developed for security tasks and was aimed at penetration testing and digital forensics. After the deprecation of BackTrack Linux in 2013, Kali Linux was released in March 2013 as a complete reboot of BackTrack Linux from top to bottom in compliance with all the Debian development standards.

Let's go through the features of Kali Linux in brief before we deep dive into this book.

Features of Kali Linux

Penetration testing tools

Kali Linux comes with more than 600 tools for penetration testing. If one were to go through the number of tools available in the predecessor that is BackTrack, there were a lot of tools which were not functional or were just duplicates of functions that were already available in other tools. These have been eliminated from the Kali Linux releases.

Free to use

BackTrack Linux was completely free of cost to use, and this has been continued with Kali Linux as well. As a Kali Linux user, you will never have to pay for the operating system or the tools it comes equipped with.

Open Source

Kali Linus is committed to the model of Open Source, and therefore the Kali Linux development tree is available to everyone on the Internet. The source code for Kali Linux is available on gitlab and is available to anyone who wants to make customizations to it and rebuild the packages to suit their specific needs.

Compliance with FHS

Kali complies with the Filesystem Hierarchy Standard, which is followed by all Linux flavors. This will make it easy for the system to locate binaries, libraries, support files, etc.

Support for wireless devices

One of the concerns with Linux systems in the past has been its support for wireless devices. Kali Linux has been developed and built in such a way that it will support a wide range of wireless devices, and it will be compatible with the hardware of a vast variety and therefore will support USB and most wireless devices.

Custom kernel

Kali Linux kernel comes equipped with the latest injection patches. As penetration testers, this helps the development team to conduct wireless assessments with ease.

They are developed in a secure environment. The development team of Kali Linux includes a very small group of individuals, and they are trusted to make commits to the repositories and packages for Kali Linux, all of which is achieved using secure protocols via multiple channels.

GPG signed

Every developer who has worked on packages for Kali Linux signs it and subsequently, the repositories sign the package as well.

Language support

Penetration tools are usually written in English. However, Kali Linux developers have ensured that Kali includes language support for users from around the world so that more users can work in their native language and find tools on Kali that they can use to complete their tasks.

Customizable

Kali developers understand enough to know that not all users can accept their interface design. Therefore, they have made it very easy for the adventurous users to customize the system as per their requirement right from the top till the kernel.

Support for ARMEL and ARMHF: ARM-based single-board devices such as the BeagleBone Black and Raspberry Pi are popular among the users, mainly because they are so inexpensive. Therefore, Kali Linux has been built in a way such that it is as robust as possible and has a fully functional installation that will support both ARMHF and ARMEL systems. A wide range of ARM devices are supported by Kali Linux and tools for ARM are kept up to date and at par with the rest of the distributions.

What's Different about Kali Linux?

Kali Linux is developed specifically to meet the needs of professionals who are looking for tools related to security auditing and penetration testing. There are several tools integrated with Kali Linux, which help meet these needs.

Single user - Root

Linux operating system usually practices operating systems that have a root user and other users with fewer privileges than the root user. Kali Linux, however, practices a single user concept that is the root with all access. This has been done because most of the tools that are required for penetration testing using Kali required high access. Thus, although most Linux flavors practice the policy to enable root access only when essential, Kali Linux use cases use the approach of using root user to decrease the burden of additional users.

Network services disabled

By default, network services are disabled on Kali Linux. Kali uses a system service that disables all network services. This helps in the installation of various applications on Kali Linux in a secure environment irrespective of the packages that are installed. Bluetooth is also blacklisted by default.

Customized kernel

Kali Linux comes equipped with a kernel that is completely customized and patched for wireless injection.

Minimal repositories

Kali Linux has minimal and trusted repositories only. Given the motive with which Kali Linux was developed, it makes absolute sense to maintain the integrity of the system. Therefore, third-party applications for Kali are kept at a bare minimum to achieve the goal of security. While many users are tempted to add third-party repositories to their sources and lists, doing so increases the risk of breaking your Kali installation.

Is Kali Linux Right For You?

Given that we are authoring a book about Kali Linux, one might expect that we recommend it to everyone in our client base to use Kali Linux. Kali Linux, however, is developed specifically for testers who are into penetration testing and those who are security specialists. Therefore, if you are just beginning to start as a Linus user, is NOT recommended at all as a system which you are looking to use as a general desktop operating system for your day to day activities such as gaming, development, web design, etc.

Kali Linux can pose as a challenge even for veteran users in the Linux domain. Kali, unlike other open source Linux projects, is not a wide-open source project, mainly because of security concerns. The development team consists of a very small number of users, and the packages that are developed for Kali Linux and committed to repositories are signed by the individual developer first and then by the entire team. Also the upstream or third party repository from which the packages are updated or new packages are pulled is very small. Adding software from repositories to your Kali operating system from third party sources that are not tested and verified by the Kali Linux team can cause harm to your system.

While the architecture of Kali Linux is highly customizable, adding random and unrelated packages that do not fit in the Kali Linux domain and are not downloaded from the regular sources will not work on Kali. Kali Linux will not support commands such as apt-add-repository, PPAs, or LaunchPad. Also if you are trying to install Steam on your Kali Linux OS, it will end up being a disaster. Installing mainstream packages like NodeJS on your Kali Linux system can also take a lot of research, time and patience. You should not begin working on the Kali Linux operating system:

- If you are just beginning to work with a Linux operating system, without having used a Linux system ever before in life

- If you do not have the basic knowledge or competence to administer a system, if you are just looking for your first Linux system to start learning Linux

- If you are just looking for an operating system to do your daily activities, Kali Linux is not the operating system that you may want to begin with

Over and above, the misuse of penetration testing tools and security within a computer network, without any authorization, may result in irreversible damage and the consequences of such damage may get you into personal or legal trouble. The excuse that "You did not know what you were doing" will not work in such cases.

In contrast, if you are aiming at becoming a professional in penetration testing with the sole goal of becoming a certified professional, there is no better operating system that you can find than Kali Linux, at any price and especially for free.

So, to summarize and answer the question we asked when we started this chapter, if you are looking to just start with the basics of Linux on Linux operating system, Kali Linux is not the deal for you. You should first begin with the simple versions of Linux such as Ubuntu, Debian, or Mint instead.

Chapter 2

Installing and Downloading Kali Linux

N ever download an image of Kali Linux from any other source than the official source. After downloading the image, always make sure to verify the SHA256 checksum value of your downloaded file with the official value of the file. It would be very easy for a third party intruder to modify the installation file such that it includes malware which will end up being hosted on your system.

You can download all official images for Kali Linux installations from the following link:

- https://www.kali.org/downloads/
- https://www.offensive-security.com/kali-linux-vmware-arm-image-download/

Where to Get Official Kali Linux Images

ISO Files for Intel-based PCs

To be able to run Kali Linux "Live" by using a USB drive on a Windows PC or an Apple PC, you will need to download a 32-bit or a 64-bit ISO image of the Kali Linux installation.

If you are unsure about what architecture of your current system, you can run the following command on the terminal in Linux or Apple OS X to know the architecture.

uname -m

If you get the response as "x86_64", it indicates a 64-bit architecture, and you can use the 64-bit ISO image available on the website (the one which has "amd64" appended to it).

If you get the response as "i386", it indicates a 32-bit architecture, and you can download the 32-bit ISO image from the website (the one that has "i386" appended to it).

You will find the architecture mentioned under the "Device Type" header in system properties on your computer.

You will find Kali Linux ISO images available for download from the website as both as a direct download file and as a torrent file.

VMware Images

If you are using VMware and want to use Kali Linux as a "guest," Kali Linux is available as a pre-built VMware machine with VMware tools already pre-installed. The image for VMware is available in 64-bit, 32-bit, 32-bit PAE formats.

ARM Images

The hardware and architecture vary considerably on ARM-based devices. Therefore, it is not possible to maintain a single image for installation across various ARM-based devices. There are a varied set of pre-built images available for Kali Linux installation across a wide set of devices.

If you want to build your ARM images, scripts for building your custom ISO are available in the Kali GitHub repository.

Verifying Your Downloaded Kali Image

Why do I need to do this?

Before you try to run Kali Linux Live or try installing it onto your machine, you need to be sure that what you have got in hand is genuine Kali Linux and not something else. Kali Linux is a professional toolkit for penetration testing. As a professional of penetration testing, you need to be confident about the tools that you are using. If your tools are not trustworthy, the investigations you do would not be trustworthy either.

Moreover, since Kali is deemed to be the pinnacle of penetration testing distributions, strengths of Kali imply that a fake version of the operating system can do a great deal of damage if it is deployed without any prior checks. Numerous people around the world who have a huge set of reasons to stick something harmful into a Kali Linux installation, and you do not want to be at the receiving end of that.

Avoiding this is simple: Make sure that you download installation images of Kali Linux only from official sources.

- https://www.kali.org/downloads/
- https://www.offensive-security.com/kali-linux-vmware-arm-image-download/

These pages are encrypted with an SSL connection, and one would not be able to access these via plain HTTPS protocol. Since this is an encrypted connection, it makes it difficult for an attacker to intercept the connection between you and the website, thus making it impossible to modify the download file.

After downloading the image file, make sure you validate that it is what you expect it to be and not a malicious file. Verifying the checksum after downloading is always a great way to ensure you have a genuine file.

There are many methods for verifying the file you have downloaded. Each provides some level of assurance and expects a particular level of effort on your part.

You can download the Kali Linux installation ISO from the "Downloads" section of the official Kali Linux website and then calculate the SHA256 checksum of the download file and compare it with the checksum listed on the website for the corresponding download file. This is a very easy method to verify the download but is sometimes susceptible to DNS poisoning. DNS poisoning implies that you are trying to resolve an official Kali Linux website, but an attacker somehow redirects you to a website they wish you to be on where the SHA checksum would show up us something else, and then you end up downloaded an infected ISO from their website.

You can also download the Kali Linux ISO via torrents. And this will also download an ISO file that will contain a SHA256 checksum. So this way you will have 2 files, one that was directly downloaded, while the other that was downloaded via torrents. You can then crosscheck if both have the same checksum using tools on Windows, Linux or Mac.

To be sure that the Kali Linux installation ISO you have downloaded is a genuine ISO and is the real thing, you can download the following files: a cleartext signature file and a version of the same file that has a signature by the official Kali Linux key and then continue to perform the following actions:

1. Use the GNU Privacy Guard (GPG) to cross-check that the signature of the cleartext file and the computed SHA256 checksum match

2. Validate that the signature in the file that has the SHA256 hash has been signed correctly with the official key.

If you are comfortable with using this complicated process to validate your downloaded ISO, you can proceed without any fear that you have got the official image of the installation for Kali Linux and that it has not been tampered with. While this is the most complex method to validate your download, it has the advantage that you have complete assurance of the integrity of your downloaded image file.

Kali Linux Default root Password is toor

Default root Password

When you are going through your Kali Linux installation, you will be prompted to set up a password for the root user. If you, however, decide to boot the operating system directly from the USB and use Kali Linux Live, the default password for the root user is "toor" without the quotes.

Chapter 3

Making a Kali Bootable USB Drive

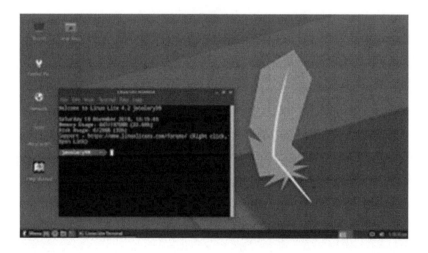

The easiest way to run Kali Linux is to run it "live" from a USB drive. The method also has a lot of advantages.

Advantages of a Bootable USB Drive

Non-destructive

It does not make any changes to your machine or your existing operating system on the machine as it runs directly from the USB drive. To go back to your existing setup without Kali Linux, you simply need to unplug the USB drive and restart your system.

Portability

You can carry the Kali Linux operating system on any USB drive in your pocket and have it running on any machine that is available to you.

Customizable

As discussed in the previous chapter, you can use scripts from the Kali Linux GitHub repository to build your custom Kali Linux installation ISO image and load it onto a USB drive as well.

Persistency

With a little bit of customization, you can make your Kali Linux Live USB drive store persistent data that will be retained across reboots.

For this purpose, we will first need to use the ISO image of Kali Linux to set up a bootable USB drive.

Requirements to create a Kali Linux USB

1. A verified copy of the Kali Linux ISO to suit the system that you intend to run or install it on.

2. If you are using Windows, you will require the Win32 Disk Imager software to create the Kali Linux USB drive. On Linux or OS X, you can use the dd command on the

terminal, which is pre-installed for creation of bootable USB drives.

3. A USB drive which has a capacity of 4GB or more. If your system supports an SD card slot, you can use an SD card as well with a similar process.

Kali Linux Live USB Install Procedure

Let's go through the procedure of creating a USB drive for Kali Linux. The process will vary as per the host system on which you are creating the USB drive depending on whether it is Windows, Linux or OS X.

Creating a Bootable Kali USB Drive on Windows

1. Plug the USB in a USB slot on your machine and note down which drive letter is designated to it. Launch the Win32 Disk Imager application that you had downloaded earlier.

2. Choose the ISO file for Kali Linux installation and ensure that you have selected the correct USB drive to be written it to. Click on Write.

3. Once the writing to the USB drive is complete, you can eject the drive and use it as a bootable USB drive to boot Kali Linux Live or install Kali Linux on your machine.

Creating a Bootable Kali USB Drive on Linux

Creating a bootable USB drive is fairly simple in a Linux operating system. Once you have downloaded your Kali Linux ISO file and verified it, you can use the dd command on the terminal to write the file to your USB drive. You will need root or sudo privileges to run the dd command.

Warning: If you are unsure as to how to use the dd command, you may end up writing the Kali Linux image to a disk drive that you did not intend to. Therefore, it is important that you are alert while you are using the dd command.

Step One

You will need to know the device path to be used for writing the Kali Linux image to the USB drive. Without having the USB drive inserted in the USB slot, execute the following command in the command prompt in the terminal window.

sudo fdisk -l

You will get an output that shows you all the devices mounted on your system, which will show the partitions as

/dev/sda1

/dev/sda2

Step Two

Now, plugin the USB drive and run the same command "sudo fdisk -l" again. You will see an additional device this time, which is your USB drive. It will show up as something like

/dev/sdb

The size of your USB drive will be written against it.

Step Three

Proceed to write the image carefully on the USB drive using the command shown below. In the above example, we are assuming that the name of your Kali Linux ISO file is "kali-linux-2019.1-amd64.iso" and it is in your present working directory. The block size parameter bs can be increased, but the ideal value would be "bs=512k".

dd if=kali-linux-2019.1-amd64.iso of=/dev/sdb bs=512k

The writing to the USB drive will take a few minutes, and it is not abnormal for it to take a little more than 10 minutes to finish writing.

The dd command will not show any output until the process is completed. If your USB drive has an LED, you will see it blinking which is an indicator of the disk being written on. Once the dd command has been completed, the output would be something like this.

5823+1 records in

5823+1 records out

3053371392 bytes (3.1 GB) copied, 746.211 s, 4.1 MB/s

This will end the processing of the equations. You can now use the USB drive to boot into Kali Linux Live or start and installation of Kali Linux on a machine.

Creating a Bootable Kali USB Drive on OS X

Apple OS X is a UNIX based operating system. So creating a Kali Linux bootable USB drive on OS X is similar to that of creating on in Linux. After downloading and verifying your copy of the Kali Linux ISO, you can just use the dd command to write the ISO to your USB drive.

Warning: If you are unsure as to how to use the dd command, you may end up writing the Kali Linux image to a disk drive that you did not intend to. Therefore, it is extremely important to be alert while you are using the dd command.

You can use the following steps to write the ISO to your USB drive.

Step One

Without plugging in your USB drive to your MAC desktop or laptop, type the following command on the command prompt of the terminal window.

diskutil list

Step Two

A list of device paths showing all the disks mounted on your system will be displayed along with the data of the partition.

/dev/disk1

/dev/disk2

Step Three

Now plug in the USB and run the diskutil list command again. You will see that the list now shows your USB drive as well. It will be the one that did not show up for the first time. Let us assume that it is

/dev/disk6

Step Four

You can unmount the USB disk from the system using the following command:

/dev/disk6

diskutil unmount /dev/disk6

Step Five

Proceed further to carefully write the Kali Linux ISO on to your USB drive using the following command. This is assuming that your present working directory is the same as that in which your ISO file is saved. The block size parameter bs can be increased, but the ideal value would be "bs=1m".

sudo dd if=kali-linux-2017.1-amd64.iso of=/dev/disk6 bs=1m

The writing to the USB drive will take a few minutes, and it is not abnormal for it to take a little more than 10 minutes to finish writing.

The dd command will not show any output until the process is completed. If your USB drive has an LED, you will see it blinking which is an indicator of the disk being written on. Once the dd command has been completed, the output would be something like this.

5823+1 records in

5823+1 records out

3053371392 bytes transferred in 2151.132182 secs (1419425 bytes/sec)

That will be the end of the processing of the equation. You can now use the USB drive to boot into Kali Linux Live or start and installation of Kali Linux on a machine.

To boot from the desired drive on an OS X machine, press the "Option" button immediately after the computer powers on and select the drive you wish to use.

Chapter 4

Installing Kali Linux

Kali Linux Hard Disk Install

Kali Linux Installation Requirements

The Kali Linux installation process is fairly simple and easy. Firstly, we need to get a machine, which has compatible hardware for the Kali Linux installation. Kali Linux supports 32-bit, 64-bit and ARM (armhf and armel) architectures. The previous sections of the book covered the process of creating bootable USB media for Kali Linux ISO. If you have a DVD drive, you can also write the ISO image to the DV to install Kali Linux on your machine.

The minimum hardware requirements to install Kali Linux on a machine are as follows.

1. A minimum disk space availability of 20 GB for the installation files.

2. A minimum RAM capacity of 1GB. Although 2GB or more is recommended for better performance.

3. A DVD drive or USB boot support to help with the Kali Linux installation.

Preparing for the Installation

You can prepare for the installation by having the following checklist ready.

1. Download Kali Linux ISO as per your system's architecture.

2. Write The Kali Linux ISO to DVD or a USB drive using the tools mentioned in the previous chapter.

3. You must ensure that your system is already set to allow a boot from a USB drive.

Kali Linux Installation Procedure

1. To begin with the Kali Linux installation, boot with the installation medium that you have created, that is DVD or USB drive. You will be prompted with the Kali Linux boot screen. You can choose either a graphical or text mode installation. It is ideal to continue with the Graphical installation.

2. Select the language that you require for the operating system followed by the country location. You will be prompted to choose the keyboard layout of your preference.

3. Enter your Geographic location.

4. The installer will then copy all installation files to the hard drive of your computer, probe all the network devices and interfaces, and then ask you to enter a hostname for your system. You can enter the hostname of your choice, and that will be the name your system will be identified with.

5. You can also enter a default domain name for your system, and this is an optional feature.

6. Enter the full name for a user who will be non-root on the system.

7. A default userid is created for the name that you have provided. You can change the username as per your choice as well if you want.

8. Select a time zone for the system.

9. Next, you will get a list of the disk on which the operating system is to be installed. You can select the entire disk otr you can use the Logical Volume Manager to create partitions if you are experienced with creating granular configurations.

10. Select the disk that you want to create partitions for.

11. You can either keep all the files on a single partition that is the default or create new partitions for a few directories of your choice depending on what you will be using the software for. If you are not sure with what you want, you

can go with the default choice, which is "All files in one partition".

12. On this screen, you have one last chance where you can have a look at all the disk configurations that you selected post which the installer will start making irreversible changes. When you click on Continue here, the installer will start with the Kali Linux installation and you will get an almost completed installation.

13. The next step is to configure the network mirrors for your system. Kali uses a central repository through which it distributes applications. If you are using a proxy server, you will need to enter that information here.

Note: If you select NO on this screen, you will not be able to use any Kali repositories for software installations in the future.

14. On this screen, you will install GRUB. Grand Unified Bootloader or GRUB is a bootloader application, which is used in case you have multiple operating systems to boot from. Given that this is a fresh installation, you can install GRUB on the master boot record and make it the primary bootloader for your system.

15. That's it. You can now click on the continue button which will reboot your system and your Kali Linux installation is now complete.

Dual Boot Kali with Windows

Kali Linux Dual Boot with Windows

Having Kali Linux installed alongside Windows on the same system can be very beneficial. Although, you need to be very patient and cautious while setting up a dual operating system installation. Firstly, make sure that all the important data from your Windows installation is backed up. Also, since this exercise will result in modification of your hard drive, it is advisable to back up everything of importance on an external media.

In the example that we are going to look at, we are using a system, which has Windows 7 already installed on it and is taking 100% of the disk space. So we will first resize the Windows partition such that it occupies less space and then proceed with installing Kali Linux on a new and empty partition.

You can prepare for the installation by having the following checklist ready.

1. Download Kali Linux ISO as per your system's architecture.

2. Write The Kali Linux ISO to DVD or a USB drive using the tools mentioned in the previous chapter.

3. You must ensure that your computer is ready to allow a boot from a USB drive.

The minimum hardware requirements to install Kali Linux on a machine are as follows.

1. A minimum disk space availability of 20 GB for the installation files on the Windows system.

2. A minimum RAM capacity of 1GB. Although 2GB or more is recommended for better performance.

3. A DVD drive or USB boot support to help with the Kali Linux installation.

Dual Boot Installation Procedure

1. To begin with the installation, boot the system using the installation media on which you have loaded the Kali Linux ISO. You will be prompted with the Kali Linux boot screen. Click on Live, which will boot you into the Kali Linux desktop.

2. Once you are on the Kali Linux desktop, launch the gparted application. We will be using gparted to compress the existing Windows partition, which will help us create sufficient space for the Kali Linux installation.

3. On gparted, select your Windows partition. There will usually be two partitions: a smaller one that is recovery partition and the larger one, which is the Windows partition. Resize the Windows partition and leave and create a new 20GB partition for the Kali Linux installation.

4. Once you have segregated your memory into the required partitions, ensure that you apply the changes to the hard drive. Exit and reboot.

Kali Linux Installation Procedure

1. The installation process here onward is the same as that mentioned in the previously in Kali Linux Hard Disk install. It only changes when you reach the partitioning section where you have to select "Guided – use the largest continuous free space" which you created using gparted earlier.

2. Upon completion of the installation, you will be prompted with a GRUB boot menu. This will now give you two options to boot into Windows or Kali Linux.

Dual Boot Kali on Mac Hardware

Kali Linux Installation Requirements

Kali with its Kali Linux 1.0.8 now supports EFI out of the box. This feature makes it very easy and simple to get Kali Linux installed on a wide set of Apple devices such as MacBook Pro, Air and Retina versions.

The model/make/year of the device will either make your experience or break your experience with the Kali Linux installation. Newer the device, the better your experience. Pre-installing the device with rEFInd will increase the odds of a successful installation on older devices.

This particular chapter will guide you to dual boot an OS X with Kali Linux alongside use rEFInd, optionally allowing you to encrypt your Kali Linux installation.

Your experience with using Kali Linux is dependent on the make, model and the year when your device was manufactured. Newer devices will work better with Kali Linux. If you have an older system, it is advised that you install rEFInd to improve the chances of success.

When we use a 3rd party software rEFInd, it helps us open up the boot menu for OS X, which is apt for dual booting. It also helps older Apple devices boot from USB, which otherwise could not. Once you have installed Kali Linux, you can customize rEFInd to hide it or remove it completely.

Installation Prerequisites

1. Minimum disk space of 20GB for the Kali Linux installation.

2. A minimum of 1GB RAM. However, it is recommended to have 2GB or higher.

3. USB boot may or may not work on devices older than 2012 without rEFInd. Therefore a blank DVD is advisable.

4. A blank DVD or a USB with 4GB or higher space for a device which is newer than 2012.

5. OS X 10.7 or higher versions.

Preparing for the Installation

You can prepare for the installation by having the following checklist ready.

1. Download Kali Linux ISO as per your system's architecture.

2. Write The Kali Linux ISO to DVD or a USB drive using the tools mentioned in the previous chapter.

3. Make sure that your computer is already set to allow a boot from a USB drive.

4. Make sure all your important data is backed up.

Preparing OSX (Installing rEFInd)

1. Download the latest copy of rEFInd on your MAC OS X

2. Run the following command:

   osx:~ mbp$ curl -s -L

   http://sourceforge.net/projects/refind/files/0.8.3/refind-bin-0.8.3.zip -o refind.zip.

   After downloading rEFInd, extract the contents of the zip file and run the install shell script with sudo.

3. Run the following command to install rEFInd

   osx:~ mbp$ unzip -q refind.zip

   osx:~ mbp$ cd refind-bin-*/

   osx:refind-bin-0.8.3 mbp$ sudo bash install.sh

4. Enter your password and let the rEFIndinstallation complete. You will see the "Installation has completed successfully" once the installation is complete.

Kali Linux Partitioning Procedure

Step One

Before we can proceed with the Kali Linux installation, we need to check if there is enough room on the hard disk. To do this, we will boot into a live Kali session and resize the partition to the required size. When the Mac boots up, immediately hold the Option key until you see the prompt for rEFInd boot menu.

Step Two

Once you see the boot menu, insert the installation medium which is the DVD or USB drive. If everything works fine, you will see two volumes.

EFI – EFI\BOOT\syslinux.efi from 61 MiB FAT volume

Windows – Legacy OS from FAT volume

Step Three

Although Kali Linux is a Debian based system, rEFInd detects it as a Windows system.

If you are using a DVD for installation, you may need to press ESC and refresh the menu once the disk is fully spinning.

If you still end up seeing only one volume, it indicates that the installation medium is not supported for your Apple device. Re-installing rEFInd and trying again would be a good option at this point just to be sure.

If you select the EFI volume, the system will hang and the boot will not continue at this time.

Step Four

If everything is fine, you can select the Windows – Legacy OS from FAT volume option, which will boot you into the Kali Linux boot screen. Here you can select Live and you will be directed to the Kali Linux desktop.

Step Five

We can now use gparted like we have read previously to compress the OS X partition and create a 20GB partition for the Kali Linux installation. Gparted can be found in Kali under:

Applications -> System Tools -> GParted Partition Editor

Step Six

Once you have gparted on, select the OS X partition. It will usually be the larger partition. Resize it and leave 20GB to create a new partition for the Kali Linux installation.

Kali Linux Installation Procedure

1. When the Mac boots up, immediately hold the Option key until you see the prompt for rEFInd boot menu.

2. Once you see the boot menu, insert the installation medium which is the DVD or USB drive. If everything works fine, you will see two volumes.

   EFI – EFI\BOOT\syslinux.efi from 61 MiB FAT volume

   Windows – Legacy OS from FAT volume

   Select Windows as Linux is identified as Windows on OS X. This will take you to the Kali Linux boot menu.

3. After reaching the boot screen, continue by selecting 'Live', Graphical Install or Text-Mode Install to begin the installation process. We will be doing this exercise with steps for the Graphical mode.

4. On the next screen, select your country location and preferred language. You will also be selecting your keyboard layout for your system.

5. The installation will begin and copy all installation files to your system's hard disk. You will then be asked to enter a hostname for your system which can be anything as per your choice. You can also enter a domain name if you have one.

6. Enter the network information as per your network. The network configuration will be picked up automatically but if

there is a DHCP service on your network, the installation may ask you to enter the network information manually. It may also happen that the installation does not detect the Network Card in which case you can install the drivers manually later.

7. Create a robust password for your system.

8. Select a time zone for your system.

9. The installer will now list down the disk choices to install Kali Linux on. We have already created a partition in the previous steps to use for the Kali installation. Select 'Guided – use the largest continuous free space'.

   If you are an experienced user, you can always use the 'Manual' option to make granular configurations. On this screen, you can also set up an encrypted LVM if you want your Kali installation to be completely encrypted.

   You will be prompted for a password now. Enter the same password that you set up during step 7 of this process. When you want to boot Kali Linux, you will need to use the same password.

   The installer will now wipe your disk securely before asking for the password. This will take some time or a few hours depending upon the size and speed of the disk.

Next we have to choose the partition structure that you want to maintain. If you want everything on a single partition, use the default option. You will be presented with an overview to which if you agree, you can click on Continue.

On this screen, you will have one last chance to review the disk configuration you have selected for your installation post which the changes would be irreversible. Click Continue and the installation will begin and you are almost done.

10. The next step is to configure the network mirrors for your system. Kali uses a central repository through which it distributes applications. If you are using a proxy server, you will need to enter that information here.

Note: If you select NO on this screen, you will not be able to use any Kali repositories for software installations in the future.

11. On this screen, you will install GRUB. Grand Unified Bootloader or GRUB is a bootloader application, which is used in case you have multiple operating systems to boot from. You can install GRUB on the master boot record and make it the primary bootloader for your system.

12. Click 'Continue' finally to finish the Kali Linux installation. We would recommend that you restart the system now. Once the system has restarted, repeat the first two steps to boot into the 'Live mode' again.

13. If your Kali Linux ISO does not include the gdisk package, it will need to be installed first.

14. If network repositories were enabled during the Kali Linux installation, you could easily install gdisk using the following commands.

apt-get update

apt-get install gdisk

This process will help us convert the Master Boot Record of the system to a hybrid such that Apple's boot manager EFI will be able to detect entries in GRUB and boot from it.

Use the following commands.

root@kali:~# gdisk /dev/sda

GPT fdisk (gdisk) version 0.8.5

Partition table scan:

MBR: protective

BSD: not present

APM: not present

GPT: present

Found valid GPT with protective MBR; using GPT.

Command (? for help): p

Disk /dev/sda: 976773168 sectors, 465.8 GiB

Logical sector size: 512 bytes

Disk identifier (GUID): 1B3DB3D4-ECFD-47A1-9435-F2FF318C2F55

Partition table holds up to 128 entries

The first usable sector is 34, last usable sector is 976773134

Partitions will be aligned on 8-sector boundaries

Total free space is 245 sectors (122.5 KiB)

Number Start (sector) End (sector) Size Code Name

1 40 409639 200.0 MiB EF00 EFI System Partition

2 409640 548413439 261.3 GiB AF00 Macintosh

3 975503592 976773127 619.9 MiB AB00 Recovery HD

4 548413440 548415487 1024.0 KiB EF02

5 548415488 958138367 195.4 GiB 0700

6 958138368 975503359 8.3 GiB 8200

Command (? for help): r

Recovery/transformation command (? for help): h

WARNING! Hybrid MBRs are flaky and dangerous! If you decide not to use one,

just hit the Enter key at the below prompt and your MBR partition table will

be untouched.

Type from one to three GPT partition numbers, separated by spaces, to be

added to the hybrid MBR, in sequence: 5

Place EFI GPT (0xEE) partition first in MBR (good for GRUB)? (Y/N): y

Creating entry for GPT partition #5 (MBR partition #2)

Enter an MBR hex code (default 07): 83

Set the bootable flag? (Y/N): y

Unused partition space(s) found. Use one to protect more partitions? (Y/N): n

Recovery/transformation command (? for help): w

Final checks complete. About to write GPT data. THIS WILL OVERWRITE EXISTING

PARTITIONS!!

Do you want to proceed? (Y/N): y

OK; writing new GUID partition table (GPT) to /dev/sda.

The operation has completed successfully.

root@kali:~#

18. We can now use both OS X and Kali Linux and we will get a choice to select which one to boot into at start up.

rEFInd Configuration

Alternatively, if you wish, you can make modifications to the rEFInd in multiple ways, which include:

1. The default Operating System selection which by default is set to OS X.

2. The Boot screen timeout value, which is 20 seconds by default.

3. Boot directly into the default Operating System selection (You can press Options during boot if you want to use a different operating system. This will open the boot menu.)

4. Remove rEFInd which implies enabling the good old Apple menu. This will still allow booting to both Apple and Kali Linux.

To make any of these modifications, just boot into OS X and modify the following file. From the terminal.

osx:~ mbp$ sudo nano /EFI/refind/refind.conf

To change how many seconds you get on the boot menu to select an Operating System, you can alter the 'timeout' value. If you set it to '-1', it will boot into the default operating system which is OS X in this case.

timeout -1

To set the default Operating System which is selected on the boot menu, modify the 'default_selection' value. OS X has the value 1 and Kali Linux has the value 2The 'default_selection' value sets the default selection on startup. OSX will be at position '1' and Kali will be at '2'. Let's use OS X as a default in this scenario.

default _value 1

Now if we save the changes we have made by modifying this file, when we reboot the system, it will feel like nothing has changed. However, if you press the Options key during boot up, the Apple boot menu will pop up and the following options will show up.

EFI Boot – OSX

Windows – Kali Linux

Recovery HD – OSX's Recovery Partition

Apple's boot menu does not let us change the values of the names of the operating systems. If you want to customize these values, you will have to go for rEFInd

Single Boot Kali on Mac Hardware

Kali Linux Installation Requirements
Kali with its Kali Linux 1.0.8 now supports EFI out of the box. This feature makes it very easy and simple to get Kali Linux installed on a wide set of Apple devices such as MacBook Pro, Air and Retina versions.

The model/make/year of the device will either make your experience or break your experience with the Kali Linux installation. Newer the device, the better your experience. Pre-installing the device with rEFInd will increase the odds of a successful installation on older devices.

This particular chapter will guide you through replacing OS X with Kali Linux on a Mac hardware device, optionally allowing you to encrypt your Kali Linux installation.

Installation Prerequisites

1. Minimum disk space of 20GB for the Kali Linux installation.

2. A minimum of 1GB RAM. However, it is recommended to have 2GB or higher.

3. USB boot may or may not work on devices older than 2012 without rEFInd. Therefore a blank DVD is advisable.

4. A blank DVD or a USB with 4GB or higher space for a device which is newer than 2012.

5. OS X 10.7 or higher versions.

Preparing for the Installation

You can prepare for the installation by having the following checklist ready.

1. Download Kali Linux ISO as per your system's architecture.

2. Write The Kali Linux ISO to DVD or a USB drive using the tools mentioned in the previous chapter.

3. Make sure that your computer is already set to allow a boot from a USB drive.

4. Make sure all your important data is backed up.

Kali Linux Installation Procedure

1. To begin with the installation, power on your Mac device and press the Options key immediately to reach the boot menu.

2. Insert the media you have created for the Kali Linux installation, that it the USB drive or DVD depending on your system. If everything is in place, you will see two options, EFI and Windows. Despite Kali Linux being a Debian based operating system it shows up at Windows on Apple.

3. Click on the Windows volume.

   Your system does not support the installation media if it does not see the Windows option. In such an event, you can install rEFInd and try the process again. Selecting the EFI volume will result in the boot process getting hung.

4. When you select Windows, the Kali boot screen will appear on your system. You can now choose either The Live

'Graphical Install' or 'Text-mode' installation method. In this book we will follow the 'Graphical Install' method.

5. On the next screen, select your country location and preferred language. You will also be selecting your keyboard layout for your system.

6. The installation will begin and copy all installation files to your system's hard disk. You will then be asked to enter a hostname for your system, which can be anything as per your choice. You can also enter a domain name if you have one.

7. Enter the network information as per your network. The network configuration will be picked up automatically but if there is a DHCP service on your network, the installation may ask you to enter the network information manually. It may also happen that the installation does not detect the Network Card in which case you can install the drivers manually later.

8. Create a robust password for your system.

9. Select a time zone for your system.

10. The installer will now list down the disk choices to install Kali Linux on. We have already created a partition in the previous steps to use for the Kali installation. Select'Guided – use the entire disk'.

If you are an experienced user, you can always use the 'Manual' option to make granular configurations. On this screen, you can also set up an encrypted LVM if you want your Kali installation to be completely encrypted.

11. You will be prompted for a password now. Enter the same password that you set up during step 8 of this process. Note that you will have to use the same password every time you boot Kali Linux.

12. The installer will now wipe your disk securely before asking for the password. This will take some time or a few hours depending upon the size and speed of the disk.

   Next we have to choose the partition structure that you want to maintain. If you want everything on a single partition, use the default option. You will be presented with an overview to which if you agree, you can click on Continue.

13. On this screen, you will have one last chance to review the disk configuration you have selected for your installation post which the changes would be irreversible. Click Continue and the installation will begin and you are almost done.

14. The next step is to configure the network mirrors for your system. Kali uses a central repository through which it distributes applications. If you are using a proxy server, you will need to enter that information here.

Note: If you select NO on this screen, you will not be able to use any Kali repositories for software installations in the future.

15. On this screen, you will install GRUB. Grand Unified Bootloader or GRUB is a bootloader application, which is used in case you have multiple operating systems to boot from. You can install GRUB on the master boot record and make it the primary bootloader for your system.

16. Click 'Continue' finally to finish the Kali Linux installation. We would recommend that you restart the system now. Once the system has restarted, repeat the first two steps to boot into the 'Live mode' again.

17. If your Kali Linux ISO does not include the gdisk package, it will need to be installed first.

18. If network repositories were enabled during the Kali Linux installation, you could easily install gdisk using the following commands.

apt-get update

apt-get install gdisk

We must now ensure that the EFI from Apple can detect and boot the GRUB. To do this, we will need to convert the MBR into a hybrid.

19. root@kali:~# gdisk /dev/sda

zsh: correct 'gdisk' to 'fdisk' [nyae]? n

GPT fdisk (gdisk) version 0.8.5

Partition table scan:

MBR: protective

BSD: not present

APM: not present

GPT: present

Found valid GPT with protective MBR; using GPT.

Command (? for help): p

Disk /dev/sda: 976773168 sectors, 465.8 GiB

Logical sector size: 512 bytes

Disk identifier (GUID): B6A4398E-3590-4BB7-AA57-D64EF74860D0

Partition table holds up to 128 entries

The first usable sector is 34, last usable sector is 976773134

Partitions will be aligned on 2048-sector boundaries

Total free space is 4077 sectors (2.0 MiB)

NumberStart (sector)End (sector)Size CodeName

 120484095 1024.0 KiBEF02

 24096 943585279 449.9 GiB 0700

3 943585280 976771071 15.8 GiB8200

Command (? for help): r

Recovery/transformation command (? for help): h

WARNING! Hybrid MBRs are flaky and dangerous! If you decide not to use one,

just hit the Enter key at the below prompt and your MBR partition table will

be untouched.

Type from one to three GPT partition numbers, separated by spaces, to be

added to the hybrid MBR, in sequence: 2

Place EFI GPT (0xEE) partition first in MBR (good for GRUB)? (Y/N): y

Creating entry for GPT partition #2 (MBR partition #2)

Enter an MBR hex code (default 07): 83

Set the bootable flag? (Y/N): y

Unused partition space(s) found. Use one to protect more partitions? (Y/N): n

Recovery/transformation command (? for help): w

Final checks complete. About to write GPT data. THIS WILL OVERWRITE EXISTING

PARTITIONS!!

Do you want to proceed? (Y/N): y

OK; writing new GUID partition table (GPT) to /dev/sda.

Warning: The kernel is still using the old partition table.

The new table will be used at the next reboot.

The operation has completed successfully.

root@kali:~#

20.That's it. You can reboot the system now and enjoy Kali Linux on a Mac hardware.

Kali Linux Encrypted Disk Install

There will be times when you are using your system to store very sensitive data and information and in such cases, it is a good idea to install Kali Linux using full disk encryption. The Kali Linux installer provides an option for LVM encrypted installation for both hard disks and USB drives. The installation process is similar to a normal Kali Linux installation process with just selecting Encrypted LVM partition during the process of installation.

Kali Linux Encrypted Installation Requirements

Installation Prerequisites

1. Minimum disk space of 20GB for the Kali Linux installation.

2. A minimum of 1GB RAM. However, it is recommended to have 2GB or higher.

3. USB boot may or may not work on devices older than 2012 without rEFInd. Therefore a blank DVD is advisable.

4. A blank DVD or a USB with 4GB or higher space for a device which is newer than 2012.

5. OS X 10.7 or higher versions.

Preparing for the Installation

You can prepare for the installation by having the following checklist ready.

1. Download Kali Linux ISO as per your system's architecture.

2. Write The Kali Linux ISO to DVD or a USB drive using the tools mentioned in the previous chapter.

3. Make sure that your computer is already set to allow a boot from a USB drive.

4. Make sure all your important data is backed up.

Kali Linux Installation Procedure

1. After reaching the boot screen, continue by selecting 'Live', Graphical Install or Text-Mode Install to begin the installation process. We will be doing this exercise with steps for the Graphical mode.

2. On the next screen, select your country location and preferred language. You will also be selecting your keyboard layout for your system.

3. The installation will begin and copy all installation files to your system's hard disk. You will then be asked to enter a hostname for your system which can be anything as per your choice. You can also enter a domain name if you have one.

4. Create a robust password for your system

5. Select a time zone for your system.

6. The installer will now list down the disk choices to install Kali Linux on. We have already created a partition in the previous steps to use for the Kali installation. Select'Guided – use the entire disk and set up encrypted LVM'.

7. Select a destination drive on which you want to install Kali Linux. In case, we are using a USB drive as the destination drive, you can use this USB drive in the future to boot an encrypted Kali Linux session.

8. Enter your preference for the partitioning scheme. For the purpose of encryption, you will need to enter a password for encryption. Note that you will have to use the same password every time you boot Kali Linux.

9. The next step is to configure the network mirrors for your system. Kali uses a central repository through which it distributes applications. If you are using a proxy server, you will need to enter that information here.

Note: If you select NO on this screen, you will not be able to use any Kali repositories for software installations in the future.

10. On this screen, you will install GRUB. Grand Unified Bootloader or GRUB is a bootloader application which is used in case you have multiple operating systems to boot from. You can install GRUB on the master boot record and make it the primary bootloader for your system.

11. Click 'Continue' finally to finish the Kali Linux installation. We would recommend that you restart the system now. If your destination drive was selected as USB drive during installation, you would need to enable USB boot from your BIOS. On boot enter the encryption password to boot into your encrypted installation of Kali Linux.

Kali Linux Network PXE Install

Setup a PXE Server

The Preboot Execution Environment (PXE) is a method that allows computers on a network which are not loaded with an operating system to be booted and configured using remote access by an administrator. PXE installations for Kali Linux can be useful from something as small as a single laptop, which does not have a CDROM or a USB port to something as huge as deployments of Kali Linux on a network of computers in an enterprise.

We begin with installing dnsmasq to have a DHCP/TFTP server and then edit the dnsmasq. Conf file.

apt-get install dnsmasq

nano /etc/dnsmasq.conf

In dnsmasq. Conf, we have to enable PXE, DHCP and TFTP booting and modify the dhcp-range to as per your network environment. Optionally, if needed, you can also modify your DNS servers and gateway using the dhcp-option parameter:

interface=eth0

dhcp-range=192.168.101.100,192.168.101.200,12h

dhcp-boot=pxelinux.0

enable-tftp

tftp-root=/tftpboot/

dhcp-option=3,192.168.101.1

dhcp-option=6,8.8.8.8,8.8.4.4

After modifying the parameters, restart the dnsmasq service for the changes to take effect.

service dnsmasq restart

Download Kali PXE Netboot Images

We will now work on creating a directory to keep the Kali Linux Netboot image and download the Kali Linux image from the website which we need. mkdir -p /tftpboot

cd /tftpboot

for 64 bit systems:

wget http://http.kali.org/kali/dists/kali-rolling/main/installer-amd64/current/images/netboot/netboot.tar.gz

for 32 bit systems:

wget http://http.kali.org/kali/dists/kali-rolling/main/installer-i386/current/images/netboot/netboot.tar.gz

Tar zxpf netboot.tar.gz

Rm netboot.tar.gz

Configure Target to Boot From Network

Once you have configured everything as mentioned, you can now boot a target system on the network and configure it to boot from the network. Your PXE server will allocate an IP address to the target system and the target system will boot Kali Linux.

Kali Linux on ARM

Kali Linux – ASUS Chromebook Flip

The ASUS Chromebook Flip is a Chromebook ARM device with the following configuration.

1. 1.8 GHz quad core processor

2. 2GB or 4GB of RAM

3. A 10 point 10.1" multitouch screen

Kali Linux can be installed on an external SD card or a USB drive.

The following instructions will help you install Kali Linux on an ASUS Chromebook Flip.

1. You will need an 8GB or higher USB drive or SD card to install Kali Linux on.

2. Enable USB boot on your Chromebook by going into the developer mode. The legacy boot can be ignored on this device since SeaBIOS is not supported.

3. Download the Kali Linux ISO from https://www.offensive-security.com/kali-linux-arm-images/ for ASUS Chromebook Flip.

4. You can now write this image to the SD card or USB drive by using the dd utility. In the example shown by us, we will be installing Kali Linux on the SD card which has the path /dev/sdb. This can be changed as per your requirement.

Note: This will erase all content on your SD card or USB drive. Choosing the wrong disk device can also result in the hard disk of the device getting wiped out.

xzcat kali-$version-veyron.img.xz | dd of=/dev/sdb bs=512k

The time taken to complete the Kali Linux installation depends on the speed of the SD card or USB drive and the size of the Kali Linux image.

After the dd operation completes, you can boot up the ASUS Chromebook Flip keeping the SD card or USB drive plugged in.

You can log in to the Kali desktop using the 'root' username and password 'toor'.

Kali on ASUS Chromebook Flip – Developer Instructions

If you like to work with software and develop some new software, and want to make some customizations to the Kali Linux image for ASUS Chromebook Flip like making changes to the configuration of the kernel, you can check our the Kali scripts for ARM devices on https://gitlab.com/kalilinux/build-scripts/kali-arm. The script to be used is Chromebook-arm-veyron.sh

Chapter 5

ARM Devices

Kali Linux – MiniX

The Mini-X is an ARM device with the following configuration.

1. 1 GHz dual-core processor

2. 1GB of RAM.

Kali Linux installation can be performed using an external SD card for Minu-X.

Kali on Mini-X – User Instructions

The following instructions will help you install Kali Linux on your Mini-X.

1. You will need an 8GB or higher SD card to install Kali Linux on.

2. Download the Kali Linux ISO from https://www.offensive-security.com/kali-linux-arm-images/ for Mini-X.

3.   You can now write this image to the SD card by using the dd utility. In the example shown by us, we will be installing Kali Linux on the SD card which has the path /dev/sdb. You can change this as per your requirement.

Note: This will erase all content on your SD card. Choosing the wrong disk device can also result into the hard disk of the device getting wiped out.

xzcat kali-$version-mini-x.img.xz | dd of=/dev/sdb bs=512k

This process can take a while depending on your device speed and image size.

The time taken to complete the Kali Linux installation depends on the speed of the SD card and the size of the Kali Linux image.

After the dd operation completes, you can boot up the Mini-X keeping the SD card plugged in. You can login to the Kali desktop using the 'root' username and password 'toor'.

Kali on Mini-X – Developer Instructions

If you are someone who is adventurous and likes to play around the development of a software and want to make some customizations to the Kali Linux image for Mini-X like making changes to the configuration of the kernel, you can check out the Kali scripts for ARM devices on https://gitlab.com/kalilinux/build-scripts/kali-arm. The script to be used is mini-x.sh.

Kali Linux – Cubietruck

The Cubietruck is an ARM device with the following configuration.

1. 1 GHz dual core processor

2. 2GB of RAM

Kali Linux installation can be performed using an external SD card for Cubietruck.

Kali on Cubietruck – User Instructions

The following instructions will help you install Kali Linux on your Cubietruck.

1. You will need an 8GB or higher SD card to install Kali Linux on.

2. Download the Kali Linux ISO from https://www.offensive-security.com/kali-linux-arm-images/ for Cubietruck.

3. You can now write this image to the SD card by using the dd utility. In the example shown by us, we will be installing Kali Linux on the SD card which has the path /dev/sdb. You can change this as per your requirement.

Note: This will erase all content on your SD card. Choosing the wrong disk device can also result into the hard disk of the device getting wiped out.

xzcat kali-$version-cubietruck.img.xz | dd of=/dev/sdb bs=512k

This process can take a while depending on your device speed and image size.

The time taken to complete the Kali Linux installation depends on the speed of the SD card and the size of the Kali Linux image.

After the dd operation completes, you can boot up the Cubietruck keeping the SD card plugged in. You can login to the Kali desktop using the 'root' username and password 'toor'.

Kali on Cubietruck – Developer Instructions

If you are someone who is adventurous and likes to play around the development of a software and want to make some customizations to the Kali Linux image for Cubietruck like making changes to the configuration of the kernel, you can check out the Kali scripts for ARM devices on https://gitlab.com/kalilinux/build-scripts/kali-arm. The script to be used is cubietruck.sh

Kali Linux – Raspberry Pi2

The Raspberry Pi2 is an ARM device, which comes with the following configuration.

1. 900 MHz quad core processor

2. 1GB of RAM

Kali Linux installation can be performed using an external SD card for Raspberry Pi2.

Kali on Raspberry Pi2 – User Instructions

The following instructions will help you install Kali Linux on your Raspberry Pi2.

1. You will need an 8GB or higher SD card or eMMC to install Kali Linux on.

2. Download the Kali Linux ISO from https://www.offensive-security.com/kali-linux-arm-images/ for Raspberyy Pi2.

3. You can now write this image to the SD card by using the dd utility. In the example shown by us, we will be installing Kali Linux on the SD card which has the path /dev/sdb. You can change this as per your requirement.

Note: This will erase all content on your SD card. Choosing the wrong disk device can also result into the hard disk of the device getting wiped out.

xzcat kali-$version-rpi2.img.xz | dd of=/dev/sdb bs=512k

This process can take a while depending on your device speed and image size.

The time taken to complete the Kali Linux installation depends on the speed of the SD card and the size of the Kali Linux image.

After the dd operation completes, you can boot up the Raspberry Pi2 keeping the SD card plugged in. You can login to the Kali desktop using the 'root' username and password 'toor'.

Kali on Raspberry Pi2 – Developer Instructions

If you are someone who is adventurous and likes to play around the development of a software and want to make some customizations to the Kali Linux image for Raspberry Pi2 like making changes to the configuration of the kernel, you can check out the Kali scripts for ARM devices on https://gitlab.com/kalilinux/build-scripts/kali-arm. The script to be used is rpi2.sh

Kali Linux – Trimslice

The Trimslice is an ARM device, which comes with the following configuration.

1. 1 GHZ dual core processor

2. 1GB of RAM

Kali Linux installation can be performed using an external SD card for Trimslice.

Kali on Trimslice – User Instructions

The following instructions will help you install Kali Linux on your Trimslice.

1. You will need an 8GB or higher SD card or eMMC to install Kali Linux on.

2. Download the Kali Linux ISO from https://www.offensive-security.com/kali-linux-arm-images/ for Trimslice.

3. You can now write this image to the SD card by using the dd utility. In the example shown by us, we will be installing Kali Linux on the SD card which has the path /dev/sdb. You can change this as per your requirement.

Note: This will erase all content on your SD card. Choosing the wrong disk device can also result into the hard disk of the device getting wiped out.

xzcat kali-$version-trimslice.img.xz | dd of=/dev/sdb bs=512k

This process can take a while depending on your device speed and image size.

The time taken to complete the Kali Linux installation depends on the speed of the SD card and the size of the Kali Linux image.

After the dd operation completes, you can boot up the Trimslice keeping the SD card plugged in. You can login to the Kali desktop using the 'root' username and password 'toor'.

Kali on Trimslice – Developer Instructions

If you are someone who is adventurous and likes to play around the development of a software and want to make some customizations to the Kali Linux image for Trimslice like making changes to the configuration of the kernel, you can check out the Kali scripts for ARM devices on https://gitlab.com/kalilinux/build-scripts/kali-arm. The script to be used is trimslice.sh

Kali Linux – Cubieboard2

The Cubieboard2 is an ARM device, which comes with the following configuration.

1. 1.4 Ghz dual core processor

2. 1GB of RAM

Kali Linux installation can be performed using an external SD card for Cubieboard2.

Kali on Cubieboard2 – User Instructions

The following instructions will help you install Kali Linux on your Cubieboard2.

1. You will need an 8GB or higher SD card or eMMC to install Kali Linux on.

2. Download the Kali Linux ISO from https://www.offensive-security.com/kali-linux-arm-images/ for Cubieboard2.

3. You can now write this image to the SD card by using the dd utility. In the example shown by us, we will be installing Kali Linux on the SD card which has the path /dev/sdb. You can change this as per your requirement.

Note: This will erase all content on your SD card. Choosing the wrong disk device can also result into the hard disk of the device getting wiped out.

xzcat kali-$version-cubieboard2.img.xz | dd of=/dev/sdb bs=512k

This process can take a while depending on your device speed and image size.

The time taken to complete the Kali Linux installation depends on the speed of the SD card and the size of the Kali Linux image.

After the dd operation completes, you can boot up the Cubieboard2 keeping the SD card plugged in. You can login to the Kali desktop using the 'root' username and password 'toor'.

Kali on Cubieboard2 – Developer Instructions

If you are someone who is adventurous and likes to play around the development of a software and want to make some customizations to the Kali Linux image for Cubieboard2 like making changes to the configuration of the kernel, you can check out the Kali scripts for ARM devices on https://gitlab.com/kalilinux/build-scripts/kali-arm. The script to be used is cubieboard2.sh

Kali Linux – RIoTboard

The RIoTboard is an ARM device, which features the following configuration.

1. 1 Ghz Cortex A9 processor

2. 1GB of RAM

Kali Linux installation can be performed using an external SD card for the RIotboard.

Kali on RIoTboard – User Instructions

The following instructions will help you install Kali Linux on your RIoTboard.

1. You will need an 8GB or higher SD card or eMMC to install Kali Linux on.

2. Download the Kali Linux ISO from https://www.offensive-security.com/kali-linux-arm-images/ for RIoTboard.

3. You can now write this image to the SD card by using the dd utility. In the example shown by us, we will be installing Kali Linux on the SD card which has the path /dev/sdb. You can change this as per your requirement.

Note: This will erase all content on your SD card. Choosing the wrong disk device can also result into the hard disk of the device getting wiped out.

xzcat kali-$version-riot.img.xz | dd of=/dev/sdb bs=512k

This process can take a while depending on your device speed and image size.

The time taken to complete the Kali Linux installation depends on the speed of the SD card and the size of the Kali Linux image.

After the dd operation completes, you can boot up the RIoTboard keeping the SD card plugged in. You can login to the Kali desktop using the 'root' username and password 'toor'.

Kali on RIoTboard – Developer Instructions

If you are someone who is adventurous and likes to play around the development of a software and want to make some customizations to the Kali Linux image for RIoTboard like making changes to the configuration of the kernel, you can check out the Kali scripts for ARM devices on https://gitlab.com/kalilinux/build-scripts/kali-arm. The script to be used is riot.sh

Kali Linux – NanoPi2

The NanoPi2 is an ARM device, which comes with the following configuration.

1. 1.9 GHz quad core processor

2. 1GB of RAM

Kali Linux installation can be performed using an external SD card for the NanoPi2

Kali on NanoPi2 – User Instructions

The following instructions will help you install Kali Linux on your NanoPi2.

1. You will need an 8GB or higher SD card or eMMC to install Kali Linux on.

2. Download the Kali Linux ISO from https://www.offensive-security.com/kali-linux-arm-images/ for NanoPi2.

3. You can now write this image to the SD card by using the dd utility. In the example shown by us, we will be installing Kali Linux on the SD card which has the path /dev/sdb. You can change this as per your requirement.

Note: This will erase all content on your SD card. Choosing the wrong disk device can also result into the hard disk of the device getting wiped out.

xzcat kali-$version-nanopi2.img.xz | dd of=/dev/sdb bs=512k

This process can take a while depending on your device speed and image size.

The time taken to complete the Kali Linux installation depends on the speed of the SD card and the size of the Kali Linux image.

After the dd operation completes, you can boot up the NanoPi2 keeping the SD card plugged in. You can login to the Kali desktop using the 'root' username and password 'toor'.

Kali on NanoPi2 – Developer Instructions

If you are someone who is adventurous and likes to play around the development of a software and want to make some customizations to the Kali Linux image for NanoPi2 like making changes to the configuration of the kernel, you can check out the Kali scripts for ARM devices on https://gitlab.com/kalilinux/build-scripts/kali-arm. The script to be used is nanopi2.sh

Kali Linux – Utilite Pro

The Utilite Pro is an ARM device, which comes with the following configuration.

1. 1.2 GHz quad core Cortex A9 processor

2. 2GB of RAM

Kali Linux installation can be performed using an external SD card for the Utilite Pro.

Kali on Utilite Pro – User Instructions

The following instructions will help you install Kali Linux on your Utilite Pro.

1. You will need an 8GB or higher SD card or eMMC to install Kali Linux on.

2. Download the Kali Linux ISO from https://www.offensive-security.com/kali-linux-arm-images/ for Utilite Pro.

3. You can now write this image to the SD card by using the dd utility. In the example shown by us, we will be installing Kali Linux on the SD card which has the path /dev/sdb. You can change this as per your requirement.

Note: This will erase all content on your SD card. Choosing the wrong disk device can also result into the hard disk of the device getting wiped out.

xzcat kali-$version-utilite.img.xz | dd of=/dcv/sdb bs=512k

This process can take a while depending on your device speed and image size.

The time taken to complete the Kali Linux installation depends on the speed of the SD card and the size of the Kali Linux image.

After the dd operation completes, you can boot up the Utilite Pro keeping the SD card plugged in. You can login to the Kali desktop using the 'root' username and password 'toor'.

Kali on Utilite – Developer Instructions

If you are someone who is adventurous and likes to play around the development of a software and want to make some customizations to the Kali Linux image for Utilite Pro like making changes to the configuration of the kernel, you can check out the Kali scripts for ARM devices on https://gitlab.com/kalilinux/build-scripts/kali-arm. The script to be used is utilite.sh

Kali Linux – ODROID-C1

The ODROID-C1 is an ARM device, which comes with the following configuration.

1. 1.5 GHz quad core Cortex A5 processor

2. 1GB of RAM

Kali Linux installation can be performed using an external SD card for the ODROID-C1.

Kali on ODROID-C1 – User Instructions

The following instructions will help you install Kali Linux on your ODROID-C1.

1. You will need an 8GB or higher SD card or eMMC to install Kali Linux on.

2. Download the Kali Linux ISO from https://www.offensive-security.com/kali-linux-arm-images/ for ODROID-C1

3. You can now write this image to the SD card by using the dd utility. In the example shown by us, we will be installing Kali Linux on the SD card which has the path /dev/sdb. You can change this as per your requirement.

Note: This will erase all content on your SD card. Choosing the wrong disk device can also result into the hard disk of the device getting wiped out.

xzcat kali-$version-odroidc.img.xz | dd of=/dev/sdb bs=512k

This process can take a while depending on your device speed and image size.

The time taken to complete the Kali Linux installation depends on the speed of the SD card and the size of the Kali Linux image.

After the dd operation completes, you can boot up the ODROID-C1 keeping the SD card plugged in. You can login to the Kali desktop using the 'root' username and password 'toor'.

Kali on ODROID-C1 – Developer Instructions

If you are someone who is adventurous and likes to play around the development of a software and want to make some customizations to the Kali Linux image for ODROID-C1 like making changes to the configuration of the kernel, you can check out the Kali scripts for ARM devices on https://gitlab.com/kalilinux/build-scripts/kali-arm. The script to be used is odroid-c.sh

Kali Linux on USB Armory

The USB Armory is manufactured by Inverse Path and is a hardware design that is open source in the form of a computer that is the size of a flash drive.

Kali Linux installation can be performed using an external SD card for the USB Armory.

Kali on USB armory – User Instructions

The following instructions will help you install Kali Linux on your USB Armory.

1. You will need an 8GB or higher SD card to install Kali Linux on.

2. Download the Kali Linux ISO from https://www.offensive-security.com/kali-linux-arm-images/ for USB Armory.

3. You can now write this image to the SD card by using the dd utility. In the example shown by us, we will be installing

Kali Linux on the SD card which has the path /dev/sdb. You can change this as per your requirement.

Note: This will erase all content on your SD card. Choosing the wrong disk device can also result into the hard disk of the device getting wiped out.

xzcat kali-$version-usbarmory.img.xz | dd of=/dev/sdb bs=512k

This process can take a while depending on your device speed and image size.

The time taken to complete the Kali Linux installation depends on the speed of the SD card and the size of the Kali Linux image.

After the dd operation completes, you can boot up the USB Armory keeping the SD card plugged in. You can login to the Kali desktop using the 'root' username and password 'toor'.

Kali on USB armory – Developer Instructions

If you are someone who is adventurous and likes to play around the development of a software and want to make some customizations to the Kali Linux image for USB Armory like making changes to the configuration of the kernel, you can check out the Kali scripts for ARM devices on https://gitlab.com/kalilinux/build-scripts/kali-arm. The script to be used is usbarmory.sh

Kali Linux on Acer Tegra Chromebook 13"

The Acer Tegra Chromebook is an ARM device which is an ultraportable laptop. Getting a Kali image that runs on the Acer

Tegra Chromebook was quite a challenge. The Acer Tegra Chromebook comes with the following configuration.

1. 2.1 GHz quad core Tegra K1 processor.

2. 4GB of RAM.

Kali Linux installation can be performed using an external SD card for the Acer Tegra Chromebook keeping the internal hard disk completely safe and untouched.

Kali on Chromebook – User Instructions

The following instructions will help you install Kali Linux on your Acer Tegra Chromebook.

1. You will need an 8GB or higher SD card to install Kali Linux on.

2. Enable USB boot and put the Acer Tegra Chromebook in developer mode.

3. Download the Kali Linux ISO from https://www.offensive-security.com/kali-linux-arm-images/ for Acer Tegra Chromebook.

4. You can now write this image to the SD card by using the dd utility. In the example shown by us, we will be installing Kali Linux on the SD card which has the path /dev/sdb. You can change this as per your requirement.

Note: This will erase all content on your SD card. Choosing the wrong disk device can also result into the hard disk of the device getting wiped out.

xzcat kali-$version-acer.img | dd of=/dev/sdb bs=512k

This process can take a while depending on your device speed and image size.

The time taken to complete the Kali Linux installation depends on the speed of the SD card and the size of the Kali Linux image.

After the dd operation completes, you can boot up the Acer Tegra Chromebook keeping the SD card plugged in. You can login to the Kali desktop using the 'root' username and password 'toor'.

Kali on Acer Tegra Chromebook – Developer Instructions

If you are someone who is adventurous and likes to play around the development of a software and want to make some customizations to the Kali Linux image for Acer Tegra Chromebook like making changes to the configuration of the kernel, you can check out the Kali scripts for ARM devices on https://gitlab.com/kalilinux/build-scripts/kali-arm. The script to be used is chromebook-arm-acer.sh

Kali Linux on ODROID-XU3

The ODROID-XU3 is an octacore ARM device which comes with the following configuration.

1. 4 A15 cores and 4 A7 cores for processing power
2. 4GB of RAM

3. It is a fast ARM device.

Kali Linux installation can be performed using an external SD card for the ODROID-XU3.

Kali on ODROID-XU3 – User Instructions

The following instructions will help you install Kali Linux on your ODROID-XU3.

1. Get a nice fast 8 GB micro SD card or eMMC to install Kali Linux on.

2. Download the Kali Linux ISO from https://www.offensive-security.com/kali-linux-arm-images/ for ODROID-XU3.

3. You can now write this image to the SD card by using the dd utility. In the example shown by us, we will be installing Kali Linux on the SD card which has the path /dev/sdb. You can change this as per your requirement.

Note: This will erase all content on your SD card. Choosing the wrong disk device can also result into the hard disk of the device getting wiped out.

xzcat kali-$version-odroidxu3.img.xz | dd of=/dev/sdb bs=512k

This process can take a while depending on your device speed and image size.

The time taken to complete the Kali Linux installation depends on the speed of the SD card and the size of the Kali Linux image.

After the dd operation completes, you can boot up the ODROID-XU3 keeping the SD card plugged in. You can login to the Kali desktop using the 'root' username and password 'toor'.

Kali on ODROID-XU3 – Developer Instructions

If you are someone who is adventurous and likes to play around the development of a software and want to make some customizations to the Kali Linux image for ODROID-XU3 like making changes to the configuration of the kernel, you can check out the Kali scripts for ARM devices on https://gitlab.com/kalilinux/build-scripts/kali-arm. The script to be used is odroid-xu3.sh

Kali Linux – CuBox-i4Pro

The SolidRun CuBox-i4Pro is the smallest computer in the world. The configuration is as follows.

1. 1 GHz quad core i.MX6 processor

2. 2GB of RAM

3. Gbit ethernet, MicroSD slot and eSata port

Kali on Cubox-i4 Pro – User Instructions

The following instructions will help you install Kali Linux on your CuBox-i4Pro.

1. Get a nice fast 8 GB micro SD card to install Kali Linux on.

2. Download the Kali Linux ISO from https://www.offensive-security.com/kali-linux-arm-images/ for CuBox-i4Pro.

3. You can now write this image to the SD card by using the dd utility. In the example shown by us, we will be installing Kali Linux on the SD card which has the path /dev/sdb. You can change this as per your requirement.

Note: This will erase all content on your SD card. Choosing the wrong disk device can also result into the hard disk of the device getting wiped out.

xzcat kali-$version-cubox-i.img.xz | dd of=/dev/sdb bs=512k

This process can take a while depending on your device speed and image size.

The time taken to complete the Kali Linux installation depends on the speed of the SD card and the size of the Kali Linux image.

After the dd operation completes, you can boot up the CuBox-i4Pro keeping the SD card plugged in. You can login to the Kali desktop using the 'root' username and password 'toor'.

Kali on SolidRun Cubox-i4pro – Developer Instructions

If you are someone who is adventurous and likes to play around the development of a software and want to make some customizations to the Kali Linux image for ODROID-XU3 like making changes to the configuration of the kernel, you can check out the Kali scripts for ARM devices on https://gitlab.com/kalilinux/build-scripts/kali-arm. The script to be used is cubox-i.sh

Kali Linux – Samsung Chromebook 2

The Samsung ARM Chromebook 2 is an ARM device which is an ultraportable laptop. Having a Kali Linux image for the Samsung Chromebook 2 was again quite a challenge but it was achieved. The configuration of the Samsung ARM Chromebook 2 is as follows.

1. 1.7GHz quad core Exynos 5800 processor

2. 4 GB of RAM

3. The Samsung ARM Chromebook 2 os a fast ARM device.

Kali Linux installation can be performed using an external SD card for the Samsung ARM Chromebook 2 leaving the internal disk safe and untouched.

Kali on Chromebook 2 – User Instructions

The following instructions will help you install Kali Linux on your Samsung ARM Chromebook 2.

1. Get a nice fast 8 GB micro SD card to install Kali Linux on.

2. Enable USB booting by putting the Chromebook in developer mode.

3. Download the Kali Linux ISO from https://www.offensive-security.com/kali-linux-arm-images/ for Samsung ARM Chromebook 2.

4. You can now write this image to the SD card by using the dd utility. In the example shown by us, we will be installing

Kali Linux on the SD card which has the path /dev/sdb. You can change this as per your requirement.

Note: This will erase all content on your SD card. Choosing the wrong disk device can also result into the hard disk of the device getting wiped out.

xzcat kali-$ver-exynos.img.xz | dd of=/dev/sdb bs=512k

This process can take a while depending on your device speed and image size.

The time taken to complete the Kali Linux installation depends on the speed of the SD card and the size of the Kali Linux image.

After the dd operation completes, you can boot up the Samsung ARM Chromebook 2 keeping the SD card plugged in. You can login to the Kali desktop using the 'root' username and password 'toor'.

Kali on Samsung Chromebook 2 – Developer Instructions

If you are someone who is adventurous and likes to play around the development of a software and want to make some customizations to the Kali Linux image for Samsung ARM Chromebook 2 like making changes to the configuration of the kernel, you can check out the Kali scripts for ARM devices on https://gitlab.com/kalilinux/build-scripts/kali-arm. The script to be used is chromebook-arm-exynos.sh

Kali Linux – Raspberry Pi

The Raspberry Pi is a pocket friendly ARM computer which is the size of a credit card. It has a low end configuration compared to other ARM devices but the affordability is what has made it popular among Linux enthusiasts.

The Raspberry Pi is powered with an SD card and will boot from the SD card when the board is switched on.

The Kali Linux image for Raspberry Pi has been loaded with minimum tools which is as per standards maintained for other ARM devices. You can, however, install the full desktop package through an upgrade using the kali-linux-fullmeta package.

Kali Linux on Raspberry Pi — Pre-built Version

The following instructions will help you install Kali Linux on your Raspberry Pi.

1. Get a nice fast 8 GB micro SD card to install Kali Linux on. We recommend a class 10 SD card.

2. Download the Kali Linux ISO from https://www.offensive-security.com/kali-linux-arm-images/ for Raspberry Pi.

3. You can now write this image to the SD card by using the dd utility. In the example shown by us, we will be installing Kali Linux on the SD card which has the path /dev/sdb. You can change this as per your requirement.!

Note: This will erase all content on your SD card. Choosing the wrong disk device can also result into the hard disk of the device getting wiped out.

root@kali:~ dd if=kali-2.1.2-rpi.img of=/dev/sdb bs=512k

This process can take a while depending on your device speed and image size.

The time taken to complete the Kali Linux installation depends on the speed of the SD card and the size of the Kali Linux image.

After the dd operation completes, you can boot up the Raspberry Pi keeping the SD card plugged in. You can login to the Kali desktop using the 'root' username and password 'toor'.

Note: All ARM images of Kali Linux are pre-configured with the same public key. So it is advisable to change the public key as soon as the installation is complete. You can do so using the following commands.

root@kali:~ rm /etc/ssh/ssh_host_*

root@kali:~ dpkg-reconfigure openssh-server

root@kali:~ service ssh restart

Kali Linux on Raspberry Pi — Custom Build

If you are someone who is adventurous and likes to play around the development of a software and want to make some customizations to the Kali Linux image for ODROID-XU3 like making changes to the configuration of the kernel, you can check out the Kali scripts for ARM devices on https://gitlab.com/kalilinux/build-scripts/kali-arm. The script to be used isrpi.sh

Kali Linux – BeagleBone Black

The BeagleBone Black is an ARM device, which is a low-cost, and runs on community-support run by developers and hobbyists. The BeagleBone Black comes with the following configuration.

1GHz Cortex-A8 processor, which includes 3D acceleration and hardware-based floating point. When it comes to power, it's comparatively lower than a desktop or a laptop, but is again popular because of affordability.

Kali Linux installation can be performed using an external SD card, which if made bootable, will be used in higher priority over the operating system, which is onboard.

The Kali Linux image for BeagleBone Black has been loaded with minimum tools which is as per standards maintained for other ARM devices. You can, however, install the full desktop package through an upgrade using the kali-linux-full meta package.

Kali Linux on BeagleBone Black – Pre-built Version

The following instructions will help you install Kali Linux on your BeagleBone Black

1. Get a nice fast 8 GB micro SD card to install Kali Linux on. We recommend a class 10 SD card.

2. Download the Kali Linux ISO from https://www.offensive-security.com/kali-linux-arm-images/ for BeagleBone Black.

3. You can now write this image to the SD card by using the dd utility. In the example shown by us, we will be installing Kali Linux on the SD card which has the path /dev/sdb. You can change this as per your requirement.

Note: This will erase all content on your SD card. Choosing the wrong disk device can also result into the hard disk of the device getting wiped out.

root@kali:~ dd if=kali-2.1.2-bbb.img of=/dev/sdb bs=512k

Note: This will erase all content on your SD card. Choosing the wrong disk device can also result into the hard disk of the device getting wiped out.

After the dd operation completes, you can boot up the BeagleBone Black keeping the SD card plugged in. You can login to the Kali desktop using the 'root' username and password 'toor'.

Note: All ARM images of Kali Linux are pre-configured with the same public key. So it is advisable to change the public key as soon as the installation is complete. You can do so using the following commands.

root@kali:~ rm /etc/ssh/ssh_host_*

root@kali:~ dpkg-reconfigure openssh-server

root@kali:~ service ssh restart

Kali Linux on BeagleBone Black – Custom Build

If you are someone who is adventurous and likes to play around the development of a software and want to make some customizations to the Kali Linux image for ODROID-XU3 like making changes to the configuration of the kernel, you can check out the Kali scripts for ARM devices on https://gitlab.com/kalilinux/build-scripts/kali-arm. The script to be used is bbb.sh

Kali Linux – HP Chromebook

The HP Chromebook is ARM device, which is again an ultraportable laptop. Having a Kali image made for this was quite a challenge as well but it was achieved ultimately. The HP Chromebook comes with the following configuration.

1. 1.7 GHz dual core Exynos 5250 processor
2. 2GB of RAM.

Kali Linux installation can be performed using an external SD card for the HP Chromebook leaving the internal disk safe and untouched.

Kali on Chromebook – User Instructions

The following instructions will help you install Kali Linux on your HP Chromebook.

1. Get a nice fast 8 GB USB drive to install Kali Linux on.

2. Enable USB booting by putting the Chromebook in developer mode.

3. Download the Kali Linux ISO from https://www.offensive-security.com/kali-linux-arm-images/ for HP Chromebook.

4. You can now write this image to the SD card by using the dd utility. In the example shown by us, we will be installing Kali Linux on the SD card which has the path /dev/sdb. You can change this as per your requirement.

Note: This will erase all content on your SD card. Choosing the wrong disk device can also result into the hard disk of the device getting wiped out.

dd if=kali-chromebook.img of=/dev/sdb bs=512k

This process can take a while depending on your device speed and image size.

The time taken to complete the Kali Linux installation depends on the speed of the SD card and the size of the Kali Linux image.

After the dd operation completes, you can boot the HP Chromebook with the USB stick plugged in. When you reach the developer boot prompt, press CTRL+U, and you will boot into Kali Linux.

Kali on HP ARM Chromebook – Developer Instructions

If you are someone who is adventurous and likes to play around the development of a software and want to make some customizations to the Kali Linux image for HP Chromebook like making changes to the configuration of the kernel, you can check out the Kali scripts for ARM devices on https://gitlab.com/kalilinux/build-scripts/kali-arm. The script to be used is chromebook-arm-hp.sh

Kali Linux – CuBox

The CuBox is an ARM computer, which is low cost and therefore, low end. Affordability is what makes it popular among enthusiasts who are more than happy to have a tiny Linux system for the cost that it comes at.

Kali Linux installation can be performed using an external SD card for your CuBox.

Stock Kali on CuBox – Easy Version

The following instructions will help you install Kali Linux on your CuBox.

1. Get a nice fast 8 GB micro SD card to install Kali Linux on.

2. Download the Kali Linux ISO from https://www.offensive-security.com/kali-linux-arm-images/ for CuBox.

3. You can now write this image to the SD card by using the dd utility. In the example shown by us, we will be installing Kali Linux on the SD card which has the path /dev/sdb. You can change this as per your requirement.

Note: This will erase all content on your SD card. Choosing the wrong disk device can also result into the hard disk of the device getting wiped out.

root@kali:~ dd if=kali-1.0.3-cubox.img of=/dev/sdb bs=512k

This process can take a while depending on your device speed and image size.

The time taken to complete the Kali Linux installation depends on the speed of the SD card and the size of the Kali Linux image.

After the dd operation completes, you can boot up the CuBox keeping the SD card plugged in. You can login to the Kali desktop using the 'root' username and password 'toor'.

Kali on CuBox – Long Version

If you are someone who is adventurous and likes to play around the development of a software and want to make some customizations to the Kali Linux image for Samsung ARM Chromebook 2 like making changes to the configuration of the kernel, you can check out the Kali scripts for ARM devices on https://gitlab.com/kalilinux/build-scripts/kali-arm. The script to be used is cubox.sh

Kali Linux – ODROID U2

The ODROID U2 is an ARM device, which has tricky hardware.

Kali on ODROID U2 – User Instructions

The following instructions will help you install Kali Linux on your ODROID U2.

1. Get a nice fast 8 GB micro SD card to install Kali Linux on. We recommend a class 10 SD card.

2. Download the Kali Linux ISO from https://www.offensive-security.com/kali-linux-arm-images/ for ODROID U2.

3. You can now write this image to the SD card by using the dd utility. In the example shown by us, we will be installing Kali Linux on the SD card which has the path /dev/sdb. You can change this as per your requirement.

Note: This will erase all content on your SD card. Choosing the wrong disk device can also result into the hard disk of the device getting wiped out.

```
dd if=kali-$vers-odroid.img of=/dev/sdb bs=1M
```

This process can take a while depending on your device speed and image size.

The time taken to complete the Kali Linux installation depends on the speed of the SD card and the size of the Kali Linux image.

After the dd operation completes, you can boot up the ODROID U2 keeping the SD card plugged in. You can login to the Kali desktop using the 'root' username and password 'toor'.

Kali on ODROID U2 – Developer Instructions

If you are someone who is adventurous and likes to play around the development of a software and want to make some customizations to the Kali Linux image for ODROID U2 like making changes to the configuration of the kernel, you can check our the Kali scripts for ARM devices on https://gitlab.com/kalilinux/build-scripts/kali-arm. The script to be used is odroid-u2.sh

Chapter 6

Troubleshooting Installations

Kali Linux installation failures

Kali Linux installation can fail due to numerous reasons. Partial or corrupt downloads of the ISO, insufficient disk space on the target system, etc. are some of the reasons die to which the Kali Linux installation can fail. In this chapter, you will learn about the common errors that are encountered and the troubleshooting that can be done. We will go through the "Red Screen" error, which is usually encountered upon failure of the Kali Linux installation which is an indicator that a problem has occurred.

The red screen reads

"An installation step failed. You can try to run the failing item again from the menu, or skip it and choose something else. The failing step is: <description of the failing item>"

If you click on continue, you will be redirected to the Debian installer main menu. On the main menu, navigate to "save debug logs":

Hitting the continue button should take you to the Debian installer main menu. From that main menu, browse to the "save debug logs".

Here, there are several methods through which you can transfer the installation log files to another system or disk. The easiest way is to start a web server on the source machine where the installation is ongoing.

You will be prompted with a screen, which has the following question with 3 options.

How should the debug logs be saved or transferred?

1. Floppy

2. Web

3. Mounted file system

Selecting the 'web' option will start a web server from which you can download or view the installation logs.

A simple web server will be started and the screen will let you know the URL from which you can access the logs.

On choosing this option, a web server is created and you can view the logs or download the logs from the URL.

DO a log analysis to understand if something is irregular. Check if you can see any error messages or warnings ,which may have been the cause of the installation failure. In this particular case, the machine on which we are installing Kali has insufficient disk space, which cause the installation to fail and this can be seen at the end of the syslinux file.

Aug 19 23:45:05 base-installer: error: The tar process copying the live system failed (only 152937 out of 286496 files have been copied, last file was).

Aug 19 23:45:05 main-menu[927]: (process:7553): tar: write error: No space left on device

Aug 19 23:45:05 main-menu[927]: WARNING **: Configuring 'live-installer' failed with error code 1

Aug 19 23:45:05 main-menu[927]: WARNING **: Menu item 'live-installer' failed.

Aug 19 23:50:23 main-menu[927]: INFO: Modifying debconf priority limit from 'high' to 'medium'

Aug 19 23:50:23 debconf: Setting debconf/priority to medium

Aug 19 23:56:49 main-menu[927]: INFO: Menu item 'save-logs' selected

Troubleshooting Wireless Drivers

The task of troubleshooting issues with respect to wireless drivers can be a bit frustrating on Kali Linux if you do not know where to look for the drivers. In this chapter, we will learn how to troubleshoot wireless issues. The most accurate and detailed source for wireless driver issues can be found at

http://www.aircrack-ng.org/documentation.htm

90 percent of the issues can be solved if you readthe documentation for Aircrack-ng. All you need to do is run the 'airmon-ng check kill' before you put your card in the monitor mode.

The error messages for wireless devices usually tell you what is going wrong and how it can be fixed. If not, you can then proceed toward Google.

Chapter 7

Real World Applications
for Kali Linux

There are a diverse number of applications for Kali Linux in the real world. Including them in a sales pitch is critical if you want to form a business model that will generate revenue for your company, which has specialists who work in the security domain using Kali Linux.

Let's talk about an example of a small business. A personal computer in the world is hacked every 10 seconds. There are a lot of people who either run their business from home or work from home. Such businesses are started with the vision of forming a reputation.

Data security is an integral part of your business if you are just beginning to work with clients. If you look up the Internet, you will easily find articles about data breaches that have been happening in small businesses in and around your area or even a college database for that matter. A little fear can be a healthy thing. Fear sells and it sells more especially today, since we are living in the digital era.

Most people who run small businesses today run their websites using Wordpress. Travel writers, photographers, etc. use Wordpress for blogging and showcasing their photography too. Activities like these require investment of time from the website owner, and all this can be lost just because of one faulty line of code in their Wordpress website. The business owner may not only lose the time that they have invested but also their customers if there is a loss of data.

There is a Kali Linux tool called 'wpscan', which we will talk about in detail later. This application scans a Wordpress code for vulnerabilities and allows you to report them to the website owner.

Another well-known Kali tool is 'nmap'. This tool helps to scan open ports on Wi-Fi connections. Open ports can be deemed to be open doors, which can be accessed by anyone with the right amount of knowledge. The open ports can be used to access data, which is critical to a business such as customer details or even credit card details.

These tools usually run via the terminal in Kali Linux. Whenever you launch one of these tools using the dropdown menu in the graphical interface, it will always redirect you to the terminal, which launches in a preconfigured root access mode in Kali. The terminal is used to run a lot of commands while using tools in Kali and you will spend most of your time on the terminal in Kali.

If you are booting Kali as a live disk and not a full install, it is recommended that the first thing you do is open up the terminal and then type the following command to update all the software.

apt-get update

This updates all the files on your system.

You can also lookup for upgraded software using the following command.

apt-get upgrade

We will now go through all the regular commands that are used on your Kali system while you're at work.

Commands in Kali Linux

- System Info

- date shows the current date and time of the system

- cal shows the current month's calendar

- uptime shows the current uptime of the system

- w shows who is online

- whoami shows the current user that you are logged in as

- finger user displays information about the user

- uname -a shows information about the kernel

- cat /proc/cpuinfo shows information about the CPU

- cat /proc/meminfo shows information about the Memory

- df -h Shows the current disk usage

- du shows the current directory space usage

- free shows usage of the swap and memory

Keyboard Shortcuts

- Enter Runs the current command that you have typed

- Up Arrow Shows the last command

- Ctrl + R Lets you partially type a command and finds the rest

- Ctrl + Z Stops the current command and you can resume it with bg in the background or fg in the foreground

- Ctrl + C Breaks the current command and kills it

- Ctrl + L Clears the terminal screen

- command | less Allows you to scroll in the terminal window using Shift+Down Arrow or Shift+Up Arrow

- !! The last command is repeated

- command !$ The last argument of the previous command is repeated

- Ctrl + A Go to the start of the command line that you are typing

- Ctrl + E Go to the end of the command line that you are typing

- Ctrl + U Erases the line before the cursor and copies it to special clipboard

- Ctrl + K Erases the line after the cursor and copies it to special clipboard

- Ctrl + Y Paste from the special clipboard that has data copied from the Ctrl + U and Ctrl + K

- Ctrl + T Used to swap the two characters just before the cursor

- Ctrl + W Delete an argument or word which is on the left side of the cursor on the current line

- Ctrl + D Exit and logout of the current session

Other Useful Commands

- apropos subject Used to list manual pages for the subject in the command

- man -k keyword Helps display man pages which contain the keyword in the command

- man command shows the man page for the command

- man -t man | ps2pdf -> man.pdf Saves the man page to a PDF file

- which command Displays the full path of the command

- time command shows how long a command took to execute

- whereis app shows all possible locations where the app is installed

- which app Shows the full path of the app that is run by default

Searching Commands

- grep pattern files Lets you search for the desired pattern in files

- grep -r pattern dir Lets you search recursively for patternin a

- command | grep pattern Lets you search for a pattern in an output from the command

- locate file To find the file in all possible locations on the system

- find / -name filename Look for the file called filename right from the root directory

- find / -name "*filename*" Look for the file containing the string called filename right from the root directory

- locate filename Assuming that you have already used the command updatedb, search for a file called filename using the locate command

- updatedb This command updates the database of all files on all file systems that exist on your root directory

- which filename Looks up the subdirectory that contains the file called filename

- grep TextStringToFind | dir Search for all files containing TextStringToFind, starting from the directory called dir

File Permissions

- chmod octal file Change the file permissions to octal. This can be found separately for user, group and world by adding 4 for read(r), 2 for write(w), 1 for execute(x)

  Example:

  chmod 777 Assigns read, write and execute for user, group and world

  chmod 755 Assigns read, write and execute for user, read and execute for group and world

File Commands

- ls Lists down content of a directory

- ls -l Lists down content of current directory in long format

- ls -laC Lists down content of current directory in long format and in columns

- ls -F Lists down content of current directory in and shows the file type

- ls -al Lists down all files including hidden files

- cd dir Changes from the current directory to dir directory

- cd Changes the directory to home directory

- mkdir dir Creates a new directory and names it dir

- pwd Displays full path of your current directory

- rm name Deletes the file or directory called name

- rm -r dir Deletes the directory called dir

- rm -r file Forcefully deletes the file called file

- rm -rf dir Forcefully deletes the dir called dir along with all its directories and subdirectories

- cp file1 file2 Contents of file1 are copied to file2

- cp -r dir1 dir2 Copies dir1 to dir2 and creates dir2 if it does not exist

- cp file /home/dirname Copies the file called file to the path /home/dirname

- mv file /home/dirname Moves the file called file to the path /home/dirname

- mv file1 file2 Renames file1 with file2

- ln -s file link To create a symbolic link link to the given file

- touch file Creates or updates a new file called file

- cat > file Directs the standard input to the file

- cat file Prints the content of the file

- more file Displays the content of the file called file page by page, and you can proceed to the next page using the spacebar

- head file Outputs the first 10 lines of the file

- head -20 file Outputs the first 20 lines of the file called file

- tail file Outputs the last 10 lines of the file

- tail -20 file Outputs the last 20 lines of the file called file

- tail -f file Outputs the content of the file called file on a real time update basis as it grows showing the latest 10 lines

Compression Commands
- tar cf file.tar files Creates an archive called file.tar which contains the files

- tar xf file.tar Extract the content from the file names file.tar

- tar czf file.tar.gz files Creates an archive called file.tar.gz which contains the files using the GZip compression

- tar czf file.tar.gz Extract the content from the file names file.tar.gz using GZip

- tar cjf file.tar.bz2 Creates an archive called file.tar.bz2 using the BZip2 compression

- tar xjf file.tar.bz2 Extract the content from the file names file.tar.bz2 using BZip2

- gzip file Compresses a given file and renames is to file.gz

- gzip -d file.gz Decompresses the file.gz file to file again

Printing Commands

- /etc/rc.d/init.d/lpd start Print daemon is started

- /etc/rc.d/init.d/lpd stop Print daemon is stopped

- /etc/rc.d/init.d/lpd status Status of the print daemon is displayed

- lpq Displays the current jobs in the print queue

- lprm Removes the jobs in the print queue

- lpc Printer control tool

- man subject| lpr Print the content of the manual page for the subject in plain text format

- man -t subject| lpr Print the content of the manual page for the subject in postscript format

- printtool Start the X printer setup interface

Network Commands

- ifconfig Print down the IP addresses for all the devices on the local machine

- iwconfig Set the parameters for wireless devices on the network interface

- iwlist Display additional information for the wireless devices which may not be shown by iwconfig

- ping host Ping a particular host and display the results

- whois domain Print the WHOIS information for a domain

- dig domain Print the DNS information for a domain

- dig -x host Fetch the reverse lookup for a host

- wget file Download a file

- wget -c file Continue a stopped download for a file

SSH commands

- ssh user@host Connect to a particular host as a particular user

- ssh -p port user@host Connect to a particular host as a particular user on a specific port

- ssh-copy-iduser@host Copy your key to a host for a user to enable passwordless login

User Administration Commands

- adduser accountname Make a new user called accountname

- passwd accountname Set password for a user called accountname

- su Login as a superuser from the current login session

- exit Stop being superuser and revert to regular user

Process Management Commands

- ps All active process are displayed

- top All running processes are displayed

- kill pid Kill a process with id pid

- killall proc Kill all processes which have the name proc

- bg Lists down all stopped jobs or jobs in the background. Can be used to resume a background job

- fg Brings the latest ongoing job in the foreground

- fg n Brings a job named n to the foreground

Installation from Source Commands

./configure

make

make install

dpkg -i pkg.deb A DEB package is installed(Ubuntu/Debian/Linux Mint)

rpm -Uvh pkg.rpm An RPM package is installed(Fedora/Redhat)

Stopping and Starting Commands

- shutdown -h now The system is shut down without reboot

- halt All processes are stopped

- shutdown -r 5 The system is shut down in 5 minutes and then rebooted

- shutdown -r now The system is immediately shutdown and rebooted

- reboot All processes are stopped and the system is rebooted

- startx X system is started

Chapter 8

Tools in Kali Linux

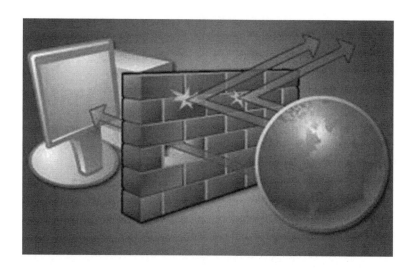

In this section we will go through the various tools available in Kali Linux for security and penetration testing. There are a number of tools in Kali which are classified as per the task that they are used for. They are as follows.

1. Exploitation Tools

2. Forensics Tools

3. Information Gathering Tools

4. Reverse Engineering tools

5. Wireless Attack Tools

6. Reporting Tools

7. Stress Testing Tools

8. Maintaining Access Tools

9. Sniffing and Spoofing Tools

10. Password Attack Tools

We will go through tools available on Kali Linux for all the categories one by one and understand the purpose of each tool and how it will help us in the security domain.

Exploitation Tools

On a network of computers, usually over the Internet, there are several web applications, which leave a system vulnerable due to bad code or open ports on the server which are publicly accessible. Exploitation tools help you to target a system and exploit the vulnerabilities in that system, thus helping you to patch a vulnerability. Let's go through all the Exploitation Tools available in Kali Linux one at a time.

Armitage

Armitage was developed by Raphael Mudge to be used with the Metasploit framework as its GUI frontend. Armitage is a tool that recommends exploits and is fairly simple to use as cyber-attack management tool which is available in the graphical form. It is open source and available for free security tool and is mostly known for the data it provides on shared sessions and the communication it provides through a single instance of Metasploit. Armitage helps a user to launch exploits and scans, get recommendations of exploits and explore the advanced features that are available in the Metasploit framework.

The Backdoor Factory (BDF)

The Backdoor Factory is a tool commonly used by researchers and security professionals. This tool allows a user to include his desirable code in executable binaries of a system or an application and continue execution of the binaries in normal state as if there was no additional code added to it.

You can install this tool on your Kali Linux system using the following commands on the terminal.

apt-getupdate

apt-getinstallbackdoor-factory

The Browser Exploitation Framework (BeEF)

The Browser Exploitation Framework is penetration testing tool built for testing exploits on the web browser. There has been an observation wherein web browsers have been targeted using vulnerabilities on the client-side. BeEF helps the user analyse these attack vectors on the client side. Unlike other tools, BeEF focuses on assessing the Web Browser which serves as an open door and it looks past the network layer and client's system.

Commix

Providing use cases for penetration tester, web developers, and researchers, Commix (short for COMMand Injection eXploiter) works in a simple environment to test web applications. It basically allows a user to find the errors, bugs or vulnerabilities with respect to command injections in web applications. This tool easily allows you to identify and exploit a vulnerability of command injection. The Commix tool has been developed using the Python language.

Crackle

The Crackle tool in Kali Linux is a brute force utility used for cracking and intercepting traffic between bluetooth devices. Most bluetooth devices have a 4-6 digit pairing code, which is in an encrypted format. Using Crackle, these codes can be decrypted if the pairing process between 2 devices is intercepted and thus allowing you to listen to all communication happening between the 2 devices.

jboss-autopwn

JBoss Autopwn is a penetration testing tool used in JBoss applications. The Github version of JBoss Autopwn is outdated and the last update is from 2011. It is a historical tool and not used much now.

Linux Exploit Suggester

The Linux Exploit Suggester tool provides a script that keeps track of vulnerabilities and shows all possible exploits that help a user get root access during a penetration test.

The script uses the uname -r command to find the kernel version of the Linux operating system. Additionally it will also provide the -k parameter through which user can manually enter the version for the kernel of the Linux operating system.

Maltego Teeth

Maltego is a tool that is used for data mining and is interactive. It provides an interactive interface that outputs graphs which help in link analysis. Since it allows link analysis, Maltego is used for investigations on the Internet to find the relationship between information that is scattered over various web pages on the Internet. Maltego Teeth was developed later with an added functionality that gives penetration testers the ability to do password breaking, SQL injections and vulnerability detection, all using a graphical interface.

sqlmap

sqlmap is a Kali tool that is open source and is used for penetration testing. It allows automating the detection of SQL injection vulnerabilities and exploiting it to take over database servers. It comes equipped with a very powerful detection engine, a range of tools which will help an extreme penetration tester and switches that help fetch information like database fingerprinting, retrieving data from databases, access to the file system of the operating system and execute commands on the operating system.

Yersinia

Yersinia is a tool that detects exploits weaknesses in network protocols and takes advantage of it. It is a tool which is a solid framework for testing and analyzing deployment of networks and systems. It comprises of layer-2 attacks which exploit the weaknesses in various layer-2 protocols in a given network thus allowing a penetration tester to detect flaws in a layer-2 network. Yersinia is used during penetration tests to start attacks on network devices such as DHCP servers,switches, etc which use the spanning tree protocol.

Cisco-global-exploiter

The Cisco Global Exploiter (CGE) tool is a security testing exploit engine/tool, which is simple yet fast and advanced. Cisco switches and routers have 14 vulnerabilities which can be exploited using the Cisco Global Exploiter tool. The Cisco Global Exploiter is basically a perl script, which is driven using the command line and has a front-end that is simple and easy to use.

Cisco-torch

The Cisco Torch is an exploitation tool which varies from the regular scanners in the sense that it can be used to launch multiple and simultaneous scans at a given point in time which results in tasks getting done faster and more efficiently. In addition to the network layer, it also helps in fingerprinting systems in the application layer of the OSI model. This is something that even a tool like NMAP doesn't provide.

Forensics Tools

We will now list down and learn tools available in Kali Linux which are used in the Forensics domain.

Binwalk

The Binwalk tool is useful while working on binary image file. It lets you scan through the image file for executable code that may be embedded in the image file. It is a very powerful and useful tool for users who know what they are doing as it can be used to detect coveted information that is hidden in images of firmware. This can help in uncovering a loophole or a hack that is hidden in the image file, which is used with the intention to exploit the system.

The Binwalk tool is developed in python and makes use of the libmagic library from python, therefore making it an apt tool for magic signatures that are created for the Unix file system. To make it even more comfortable for testers in the investigation domain, it contains a database of signatures that are commonly found in firmware around the world. This makes it a convenient tool to detect anomalies.

Bulk-extractor

The bulk-extractor tool is an interesting tool used by investigators who want to fetch specific data from a digital file. The tools helps retrieve URLs, email addresses, credit/debit card numbers, etc. The tools can be used to scan through files, directories and even images of disks. The best part is that even if the data is corrupted partially or in a compressed format, the tool will still reach its depth to find the data.

Another interesting feature of this tool is that if there is data that you keep finding repeatedly, such as email addresses, URLs, you can create a search pattern for them, which can be displayed in the form of a histogram. It also ends up creating a list of words that are found in a given set of data that may be used to crack a password for files that have been encrypted.

Chkrootkit

The chkrootkit tool is usually used in a live boot scenario. It is used locally to check the host machine for any rootkits that may be installed on the host. It therefore helps in the hardening of a system, thus ensuring that the system is not compromised and vulnerable to a hacker.

The chkrootkit tool also has the ability to scan through system binaries for any modifications made to the rootkit, temporary deletion, string replacements, and latest log deletions made. These are just a few of the things that this little tool can do. It looks like a fairly simple tool but the power it possesses can be invaluable to a forensic investigator.

p0f

The p0f tool can help the user know the operating system of a host that is being targeted just by intercepting the transmitted packages and examining them and it does this irrespective of whether the targeted host is behind a firewall or not. The use of p0f does not lead to any increase in network traffic, no lookup of names, and no probes that may be found to be mysterious. Given all these features, p0f in the hands of an advanced user, can help detect presence of firewalls, use of NAT devices, and presence of load balancers as well.

pdf-parser

The pdf-parser tool is used in parsing PDF files to classify elements that are used in the file. The output of the tool on a PDF file will not be a PDF file. One may not recommend it for textbook cases of PDF parsers but it does help to get the job done. Mostly, its use case is PDF files, which you may suspect of being embedded with scripts in them.

Dumpzilla

The Dumpzilla tool is a tool that is developed in python. The purpose of this tool is to extract all information that may be of interest to forensics from web browsers like Seamonkey, Mozilla Firefox and Iceweasel.

ddrescue

The ddrescue tool is a savior of a tool. It helps in copying data from one block device such as a hard disc or a CD ROM to another block device. But the reason it is a savior is because it copies the good parts first to avoid any read errors on the source.

The ddrescue tool's basic operation is completely automatic which means that once you have started it, you do not need to wait for any prompts like an error, wherein you will need to stop the program or restart it.

By using the mapfule feature of the tool, data will be recovered in an efficient fashion as it will only read the blocks that are required. You also get the option to stop the ddrescue process at any time and resume it again later from the same point.

Foremost

Have you ever deleted files on purpose or by mistake and realized that you needed them later? The Foremost tool is there to your rescue. This tool is an open source package which is easy to use and helps you retrieve data off of disks that may have been formatted. It may not help recover the filename but the will recover the data it held. A magical feature is that even of the directory information is lost, it can help retrieve data by referencing to the header or footer of the file, making it a fast and reliable tool for data recovery.

An interesting piece of fact is that Foremost was developed by special agents of the US Air Force.

Galleta

The Galleta tool helps you parse a cookie trail that you have been following and convert it into a spreadsheet format, which can be exported for future reference.

Cookies can be evidence in a case of cyber-crime and it can be a challenging task to understand them in their original format. The Galleta tool comes handy here as it helps in structuring data that is retrieved from cookie trails, which then can be run through other software for deeper analysis. The inputs for these analysis software need the date to be in a spreadsheet format, which is where the Galleta tool proves to be very useful.

Volatility

When it comes to memory forensics, Volatility is a very popular tool. Developed in the python language, this tool facilitates the extraction of data from volatile memory such as RAM. It is compatible with 32 bit and 64 bit architectures of almost all Windows variants and limited flavors of Linux and Android. The tool accepts memory dumps in various formats such as crash dumps, raw memory dumps, hibernation files, virtual snapshots, etc. The tool allows you to get an idea of the run-time state of the host machine and is independent of the investigation of the host.

Password that are decrypted during run-time are stored in the RAM. Thus by retrieving the details of a password, Volatility comes as a savior for investigation of files that lie on the hard disk and may be encrypted with a password. This helps in decreasing the overall time that may be required for a particular case to be investigated.

Autopsy

Sleuth Kit is a digital forensics toolkit which is open source and can be used with a wide range of file systems such as FAT, NTFS, EXT2, EXT3(and raw images) to perform analysis that can be in depth. The graphical interface developed for Sleuth Kit (which is a command line tool) is called Autopsy. Autopsy brags of features such as Hash Filtering, Timeline analysis, File System analysis and searching for keywords. It is also very versatile as it lets you add other modules to the existing set for extended functionality.

You get the option to launch a fresh new case or use one which already exists when you launch the Autopsy tool.

Xplico

Xplico is a forensic tool, which is open source and is used for network forensics. If you wish to extract data from applications that use the network protocols or Internet, Xplico is the tool for you. All popular network protocols such as HTTPS, POP, SMTP, IMAP, SIP, UDP, TCP and others are supported by Xplico. It supports both IPv4 and IPv6. An SQLite database is used to store the output data from the tool.

Information Gathering Tools

The beginning of any attacks initiates from the stage of information gathering. When you gather as much information about the target, the attack becomes an easy process. Having information about the target also results in a higher success rate of the attack. A hacker finds all kinds of information to be helpful.

The process of information gathering includes:

1. Gathering information that will help in social engineering and ultimately in the attack

2. Understanding the range of the network and computers that will be the targets of the attack

3. Identifying and understanding all the complete surface of the attack i.e. processes and systems that are exposed

4. Identifying the services of a system that are exposed, and collecting as much information about them as possible

5. Querying specific service that will help fetch useful data such as usernames

We will now go through Information Gathering tools available in Kali Linux one by one.

Nmap and Zenman

Ethical hacking is a phase in Kali Linux for which the tools NMap and ZenMap are used. NMap and ZenMap are basically the same tool. ZenMap is a Graphical Interface for the NMap tool which works on the command line.

The NMap tool which is for security auditing and discovery of network is a free tool. Apart from penetration testers, it is also used by system administrators and network administrators for daily tasks such as monitoring the uptime of the server or a service and managing schedules for service upgrades.

NMap identifies available hosts on a network by using IP packets which are raw. This also helps NMap identify the service being hosted on the host which includes the name of the application and the version. Basically, the most important application it helps identify on a network is the filter or the firewall set up on a host.

Stealth Scan

The Stealth scan is also popularly known as the hal open scan or SYN. It is called the half open scan because it refrains from completing the usual three-way handshake of TCP. So how it works is a SYN packet is sent by an attacker to the target host. The target host will acknowledge the SYN and sent a SYN/ACK in return. If a SYN/ACK is received, it can be safely assumed that the connection to the target host will complete and the port is open and listening on the target host. If the response received is RST instead, it is safe to assume that the port is close or not active on the target host.

acccheck

The acccheck tool was developed has an attack tool consisting of a password dictionary to target Windows Authentication processes which use the SMB protocol. The accccheck is basically a wrapper script which is injected in the binary of 'smbclient' and therefore depends on the smbclient binary for execution.

Server Message Block (SMB) protocol is an implementation of Microsoft for file sharing over a network and is popularly known as the Microsoft SMB Protocol.

It was then extended to the SMB "Inter-Process Communication" (IPC) system which implements named pipes and was one of the first inter process services that programmers got access to and which served as a means of inheritance for multiple services for authentication as they would all use the same credentials as that which were keyed in for the very first connection to the SMB server.

Amap

Amap is a scanning too of the next generation that allows a good number of options and flags in its command line syntax making it possible to identify applications and processes even if the ports that they are running on are different.

For example, a web server by default accepts connections on port 80. But most companies may change this port to something else such as 1253 to make the server secure. This change would be easily discovered by Amap.

Furthermore, if the services or applications are not based on ASCII, Amap is still able to discover them. Amap also has a set of interesting tools, which have the ability to send customized packets which will generate specific responses from the target host.

Amap, unlike other network tools is not just a simple scanner, which was developed with the intention of just pinging a network to detect active hosts on the network. Amap is equipped with amapcrap, which is a module that sends bogus and completely random data to a port. The target port can be UDP, TCP, SSL, etc. The motive is to force the target port to generate a response.

CaseFile

We discussed about Maltego in the previous chapters. CaseFile is known as the younger sibling of Maltego. Casefile has the same ability as Maltego to create graphs but it cannot run transforms on it. Although, you can quickly add data and then link and analyze it using CaseFile. The CaseFile tool is for investigators who work on data that is fetched from offline sources since the data they require can be queried by automation or programming. These are investigators who are getting their data from other team members and are using that data to build an information map based on their investigation.

A huge number of Maltegousers were using Maltego to try and build graphical data from offline investigations and that is how CaseFile was born. Since there was no need of the transform provided by Maltego and the real need was just the graphing capability of Maltego in and more flexible way, CaseFile was developed.

CaseFile, being an application of visual intelligence, helps to determine the relationships, connections and links in the real world between information of different types. CaseFile lets you understand the connections between data that may apart from each other by multiple degrees of separation by plotting the relationships between them graphically. Additionally, CaseFile comes bundled with many more entities that are useful in investigations making it a tool that is efficient. You can also add your custom entities to CaseFile, which allows you to extend this tool to your own custom data sets.

braa

Braa is a tool that is used for scanning mass Simple Network Management Protocol (SNMP). The tool lets you make SNMP queries, but unlike other tools which make single queries at a time to the SNMP service, braa has the capability to make queries to multiple hosts simultaneously, using one single process. The advantage of braa is that it scans multiple hosts very fast and that too by using very limited system resources.

Unlike other SNMP tools, which require libraries from SNMP to function, braa implements and maintains its own stack of SNMP. The implementation is very complex and dirty. Supports limited data types, and cannot be called up to standard in any case. However braa was developed to be a fast tool and it is fast indeed.

dnsmap

dnsmap is a tool that came into existence originally in 2006 after being inspired from the fictional story "The Thief No One Saw" by Paul Craig.

A tool used by penetration testers in the information gathering stage, dnsmap helps discover the IP of the target company, domain names, netblocks, phone numbers, etc.

Dnsmap also helps on subdomain brute forcing which helps in cases where zone transfers of DNS do not work. Zone transfers are not allowed publicly anymore nowadays which makes dnsmap the need of the hour.

DotDotPwn

The dotdotpwn tool can be defined simply to call it a fuzzer. What is a fuzzer? A fuzzer is a testing tool that targets software for vulnerabilities by debugging and penetrating through it. It scans the code and looks for flaws and loopholes, bad data, validation errors, parameters that may be incorrect and other anomalies of programming.

Whenever an anomaly is encountered by the software, the software may become unresponsive, making way for the flaws to give an open door to an attack. For example, if you are an attacker whose target is a company's web server, with the help of dotdotpwn, you will be able to find a loophole in the code of the web server. Perhaps there has been a latest HTTP update on the server overnight. Using a fuzzer on the web server shows you there is an exploit with respect to data validation which leaves an open door for a DoS attack. You can now exploit this vulnerability, which will make the server crash and server access will be denied to genuine employees of the company. There are many such errors that can be discovered using a fuzzer and it is very common for technology to have error when it releases something new in the market and it takes time to identify the error and fix it.

Another example would be an attack with respect to SQL called SQLi where 'i' stands for injection. SQL injection attacks are achieved by injecting SQL database queries through web forms that are available on a website. The conclusion is that software will always be vulnerable allowing attackers to find a way to break their way into the system.

Fierce

Fierce is a Kali tool which is used to scan ports and map networks. Discovery of hostnames across multiple networks and scanning of

IP spaces that are non-contiguous can be achieved by using Fierce. It is a tool much like Nmap but in case of Fierce, it is used specifically for networks within a corporate.

Once the target network has been defined by a penetration tester, Fierce runs a whole lot of tests on the domains in the target network and retrieves information that is valuable and which can be analyzed and exploited by the attacker.

Fierce has the following features.

- Capabilities for a brute-force attack through custom and built-in test list

- Discovery of nameservers

- Zone transfer attacks

- Scan through IP ranges both internal and external

- Ability to modify the DNS server for reverse host lookups

Wireshark

Wireshark is a kali too that is an open source analyzer for network and works on multiple platforms such as Linux, BSD, OS X and Windows.

It helps one understand about the functioning of a network thus making it of use in government infrastructure, education industries and other corporates.

It is similar to the tcpdump tool, but WIreshark is a notch above as it has a graphical interface through which you can filter and organize the data that has been captured, which means that it takes less time to analyze the data further. There is also an only text based version known as tshark, which has almost the same amount of features.

Wireshark has the following features.

- The interface has a user-friendly GUI

- Live capture of packets and offline analysis

- Support for Gzip compression and extraction

- Inspection of full protocol

- Complete VOiP analysis

- Supports decryption for IPsec, Kerberos, SSL/TLS, WPA/WPA2

URLCrazy

URLCrazy is a Kali tool that can that tests and generates typos and variations in domains to target and perform URL hijacking, typo squatting and corporate espionage. It has a database that can generate variants of up to 15 types for domains, and misspellings of up to 8000 common spellings. URLCrazy supports a variety of keyboard layouts, checks if a particular domain is in use and figures how popular a typo is.

The Harvester

The Harvester is a Kali tool that is not your regular hacking tool. Whenever there is a mention of hacking tools that are implemented using the command line, one usually thinks of tools like Nmap, Reaver, Metasploit and other utilities for wireless password cracking. However, the harvester refrains from using algorithms that are advanced to break into firewalls, or crack passwords, or capture the data of the local network.

Instead, the Harvester simply gathers publicly available information such as employee names, email addresses, banners, subdomains and other information in the same range. You may wonder as to why it collects this data. Because this data is very useful in the primary stage of information gathering. All this data helps study and understand the target system which makes attacking easier for the hacker or the penetration tester.

Furthermore, it helps the attacker understand as to how big and Internet footprint the target has. It also helps organizations to know how much publicly available information their employees have across the Internet. The latest version of the Harvester has updates which lets it keep intervals between the requests it makes to pages on the Internet, improves search sources, plotting of graphs and statistics, etc.

The Harvester crawls through the Internet as your surrogate, looking for information on your behalf as long as the criteria provided by you matches the information on the Internet. Given that you can also gather email addresses using the Harvester, this tool can be very useful to a hacker who is trying to penetrate an online login by gaining access to the email account of an individual.

Metagoofil

Metagoofil is a kali tool that is aimed at fetching publicly available such as pdf, xls, doc, ppt, etc. documents of a company on the Internet.

The tool makes a Google search to scan through documents and download them to the local machine. It then extracts the metadata of the documents using libraries such as pdfminer, hachoir, etc. It then feeds the information gathering process with the results of its report which contains usernames, server or machine names and software version which helps penetration testers with their investigation.

Miranda

Miranda is a Kali tool that is actively or passively used to detect UPnP hosts, its services, its devices and actions, all through on single command. The Service state parameters and their associated actions are correlated automatically and are then processed as input/output variables for every action. Miranda uses a single data structure to store information of all the hosts and allows you access to that data structure and all its contents.

Let's discuss what exactly UPnP is. Universal Plug and Play or UPnP is a protocol for networking that allows devices on the network such as computers, printers, routers mobile devices, etc. to discover each other seamlessly over a network and established services between them for sharing of data, entertainment and other communication. It is ideally for networks inside a private residence as opposed to corporate infrastructure.

Ghost Phisher

Ghost Phisher is a Kali tool, which is used as an attack software program and also for security auditing of wired and wireless networks. It is developed using the Python programming language and the Python GUI library. The program basically emulates access points of a network therefore, deploying its own internal server into a network.

Fragroute

Fragroute is a Kali tool that is used for intercepting, modifying and rewriting traffic that is moving toward a specific host. Simply put, the packets from attacking system known as frag route packets are routed to the destination system. It is used for bypassing firewalls mostly by attackers and security personnel. Information gathering is a well-known use case for fragroute as well which used by penetration testers who use a remote host, which is highly secured.

Masscan

Masscan is a Kali tool, which is used by penetration testers all around the world and has been in the industry for a long time. It is a tool of reconnaissance which has the capability to transmit up to 10 million packets every second. The transmission used by masscan is asynchronous and it has custom stack of TCP/IP. Therefore, the threads used for sending and receiving packets are unique.

Masscan is used to simultaneously attack a large number of hosts and that too quickly. The tool developer claims that masscan can scan the entire Internet in 6 minutes. Given its super high transmission rate, it has a use case in the domain of stress testing as well.

However, to achieve those high transmission rates, special drives and NICs are required. The communication of the tool with the users is very similar to that between the user and the Nmap tool.

Feature of masscan are as follows.

- It can be used to enumerate the whole Internet

- It can be used to enumerate a huge number of hosts

- Various subnets within an organization can be enumerated

- It can be used for random scanning and fun on the Internet

Reverse Engineering tools

We can learn how to make and break things from something as simple as a Lego toy to a car engine simply by dismantling the parts one by one and then putting them back together. This process wherein we break things down to study it deeply and further improve it is called Reverse Engineering.

The technique of Reverse Engineering in its initial days would only be used with hardware. As the process evolved over the years, engineers started applying it to software, and now to human DNA as well. Reverse engineering, in the domain of cyber security helps understand that if a system was breached, how the attacker entered the system and the steps that he took to break and enter into the system.

While getting into the network of a corporate infrastructure, attackers endure that they are utilizing all the tools available to them in the domain of computer intrusion tools. Most of the attackers are funded and skilled, and have a specific objective for an attack towards which they are highly motivated. Reverse Engineering empowers us to put up a fight against such attackers in the future. Kali Linux comes equipped with a lot of tools that are useful in the process of reverse engineering in the digital world. We will list down some of these tools and learn their use.

Apktool

Apktool is a Kali Linux tool that is used in the process of reverse engineering. This tool has the ability to break down resources to a form that is almost the original form and then recreate the resource by making adjustments. It can also debug code that is small in size,step by step. It has a file structure, which is project-like, thus making it easy to work with an app. Using apktool you can also automate tasks that are repetitive in nature like the building of an apk.

Dex2jar

Dex2jar is a Kali tool which is a lightweight API and was developed to work with the Dalvik Executable that is the .dex/.odex file formats. The tool basically helps to work with the .class files of Java and Android.

It has the following components.

- Dex2jar has an API, which is lightweight similar to that of ASM.

- dex-translator component does the action of converting a job. It reads instructions from dex to the dex-ir format and converts it to ASM format after optimizing it.

- Dex-ir component, which is used by the dex-translator component basically represents the dex instructions.

- dex-tools component works with the .class files. It is used for tasks such as modifying an apk, etc.

diStorm3

diStorm is a Kali tool which is an easy to use decomposer library and is lightweight at the same time. Instructions can be disassembled in 16 bit, 32 bit and 64 bit modes using diStorm. It is also popular amongst penetration testers as it is the fast disassembler library. The source code, which depends on the C library is very clean, portable, readable and independent of a particular platform which allows it to be used in embedded modules and kernel modules.

diStorm3 is the latest version which is backward compatible with diStorm64's old interface. However, using the new header files is essential.

edb-debugger

edb debugger is a Kali tool which is the Linux equivalent for the popular Windows tool called "Olly debugger." It is a debugging tool with modularity as one of its main goals. Some of its features are as follows.

- An intuitive Graphical User InterfaceI

- All the regular debugging operations such as step-into, step-over, run and break

- Breakpoints for conditions

- Basic analysis for instructions

- View or Dump memory regions

- Address inspection which is effective

- Generation and import of symbol maps

- Various available plugins

- The core that is used for debugging is integrated as a plugin so that it can be replaced when needed as per requirement.

- The view of the data dump is in tabbed format. This feature allows the user to open several views of the memory at a given time while allowing you to switch between them

Jad Debugger

Jad is a Kali Linux tool that is a Java decompiler and the most popular one in the world. It is a tool, which runs on the command line and is written in the C++ language. Over the years, there have been many graphical interfaces which have been developed which run Jad in the background and provide a comfortable front end to the users to perform tasks such as project management, source browsing, etc. Kali Linux powers Jad in its releases to be used for Java application debugging and other processes of reverse engineering.

Javasnoop

JavaSnoop is a tool developed by Aspect Security tool for Kali Linux that allows testing of Java application security. By developing JavaSnoop, Aspect has proved how it is a leader in the security industry in providing verification services for all applications and not just web based applications.

JavaSnoop allows you to begin tampering with method calls, run customized code or sit back and see what's going on the system by just attaching an existing process such as a debugger.

OllyDbg

OllyDbg is a Kali Linux tool, which is a debugger at a level of a 32 bit Assembler developed for Microsoft Windows. What makes it particularly useful is its emphasis on code that is in binary in times when the source is not available.

OllyDbg brags of the following features.

- Has an interactive user interface and no command line hassle

- Loads and debugs DLLs directly

- Allows function descriptions, comments and labels to be defined by the user

- No trash files in the registry or system directories post installation

- Can be used to debug multi threaded applications

- Many third party applications can be integrated as it has an open architecture

- Attaches itself to running programs

Valgrind

Valgrind is a tool in Kali Linux tool, which is used for profiling and debugging Linux based systems. The tool allows you to manage threading bugs and memory management bugs automatically. It helps eliminate hours that one would waste on hunting down bugs and therefore, stabilizes the program to a very great extent. A program's processing speed can be increased by doing a detailed profiling on the program by using Valgrind too.suite for debugging and profiling Linux programs. The Valgrind distribution has the following production quality tools currently.

- Memcheck which detects errors in memory

- DRD and Helgrind which are two other thread error detectors

- Cachegrind which is a branch prediction and cache profiling tool

- Callgrind which branch detection profile and a call graph generating cache profiler

- Massif which profiles heaps

Three experimental tools are also included in the Valgrind distribution

- SGCheck which detector for stack or global array overrun

- DHAT which is a second profiler for heap and helps understand how heap blocks are being used

- BBV which basic block vector generator

Reverse Engineering plays an important role where manufacturers are using it to sustain competition from rivals. Other times reverse engineering is used to basically figure out flaws in software and re-build a better version of the software. Kali Linux provides tools, which are known in the reverse engineering domain. In addition tools that we have discussed, there are many 3rd party reverse engineering tools as well but the ones we have discussed come installed in the Kali Linux image.

Wireless Attack Tools

In this chapter, we will look at various tools that are available in Kali Linux, which can be used for penctrating wireless devices and other devices which are accessible through wireless networks.

Aircrack

Aircrack is a Kali Linux tool, which is used for cracking passwords wirelessly and is the most popular tool in the world for what it does. It is used for cracking keys of 802.11 WEP and WPA-PSK around the world. It tries to figure out the password from the packets that are being transmitted by analyzing the packets that were caught by it initially. It can also recover the password or crack the password of a network by implementing FMS attacks that are standard in nature by optimizing the attack to some extent. PTW attacks and KoreK attacks are some of the optimizations used as make the attack work faster than other tools, which are used for cracking WEP passwords. Aircrack is a very powerful tool and is used the most all over the world.

The interface it offers is in console format. The company that has manufactured Aircrack offers online tutorials to get hands on experience.

AirSnort

AirSnort is another Kali Linux tool which is used for cracking passwords of wireless LANS and is very popular. Wi-Fi802.11b network's WEP keys can be cracked by using AirSnort. This tool basically monitors the packets that are being transmitted on the network passively. When it has sufficient packets, it computes the encryption key from the packets it has gathered. AirSnort is available for free on both Linux and Windows platforms and is fairly simple to use as well. The tool has not seen any development or updates in 3 years but the company, which created the tool is now looking to develop and maintain it further. The tool due to its direct involvement in cracking WEP is popular around the globe.

Kismet

Kismet is another Kali Linux tool, which is basically used in troubleshooting issues on wireless networks. It can be used with any wi-fi device, which supports rfmon, which is a monitoring mode. It is available on most of the platforms, which include Linux, Windows, OS X and other BSD platforms. Kismet again collects packets passively to understand the network standard and can also detect networks that are hidden in nature. It is built on the client-server architecture and it can sniff traffic from802.11b, 802.11a, 802.11g, and 802.11n. It supports the recent wireless standards, which are faster as well.

Cain & Able

Cain & Able is Kali Linux tool that is popular amongst penetration testers for its ability to crack wireless networks. The tool was originally developed to intercept traffic on a network. Later developments turned it into a tool, which could brute force its way into cracking passwords of wireless networks. The tool analyzes routing protocols of a network and helps in finding the passwords of the network. This is another popular tool used for cracking wireless network passwords. This tool was developed to intercept the network traffic and then use the brute forcing to discover the passwords.

Fern WiFi Wireless Cracker

Fern Wi-Fi Wireless Cracker is another Kali Linux tool that is very helpful with respect to network security. The tool helps you identify hosts by monitoring all network traffic in real time. The tool was initially developed to detect flaws on networks and fix the flaws that were detected. The tool is available on Linux, Windows and Apple platforms.

CoWPAtty

CoWPAtty is another Kali Linux too that is used for cracking passwords of wireless networks. It cracks passwords of the WPA-PSK networks using an automated dictionary attack. It maintains a database, which contains thousands of passwords which it uses during the attack. The chances of the tool cracking the password are very high if the password is there in its database. The drawback is that the speed of the tool can be slow and it depends on the password strength and the number of words in its database. The fact that the tool uses SHA1 algorithm with a seed of SSID is another reason for its slow speed. What this means is that thee SSIM of the password will be different. Thus the rainbow table of the tool may be ineffective while being used for the access points. Therefore, for each word that is being used for the SSID, the password dictionary of the tool generates a hash for each word. The tool is fairly simple to use with a list of commands that are to be used.

The newer versions of CoWPAtty use hash files which are pre computed and therefore the time used for computation during the process of cracking is brought down significantly, resulting in increasing the speed of the process. The hash file which is pre computed already contains 172000 dictionary files which contain at least 1000 of the most popular SSIDs. It is important for your SSID to be in that list for the attack to be successful. If the SSID is not in that list, you are just plain unlucky.

Airjack

Airjack is a Kali Linux too which is used for packet injection in Wi-Fi 802.11. DOS and MIM attacks are a specialty of this tool. This tool forces the network to give a denial of service by injecting bogus packets into the network. The tool can also help create a man in the middle attack in a given network. The tool is both powerful and popular among users.

WepAttack

WepAttack is another Kali Linux tool built on open source platform for breaking keys of 802.11 WEP. It maintains a dictionary of millions of words, which it uses to crack the password of a network. The only requirement to perform an attack using WepAttack is a WLAN card that is in a working condition. The usability of WepAttack is very limited but it works amazingly well on WLAN cards that are supported.

Wifiphisher

Wifiphisher is a Kali Linux tool, which is again used to crack the password of a wireless network. The tool steals passwords of a wireless network by executing fast paced phishing attacks. Kali

Linux has Wifiphisher pre-installed on it. It is a tool that is available on Linux, Windows and MAC and completely free to use.

Reaver

Reaver is an open-source Kali Linux tool, which is used for creating attacks which are brute force in nature against WPS. The tool is used to crack the passwords WPA/WPA2 encryptions. The tool is hosted on code developed by Google and there are high chances that the tool will be taken down if there is no local backup made for it. The last time Reaver was updated was about 4 years ago. It is a good to have tool, in addition to all the other password cracking tools that a penetration tester may want to have as it uses the same attack method.

Wifite

Wifite is also a Kali Linux tool which helps crack networks that are encrypted with WPS via reaver. It works on all Linux based operating systems. Many features related to cracking passwords are offered by Wifite.

WepDecrypt

WepDecrypt is Kali Linux tool written in C language to target wireless networks. It performs a dictionary attack and tries to guess WEP keys. Additionally it also uses key generators and performs distributed network attacks and other methods to figure out the key of a wireless network. It depends on a few libraries to function. It i snot a very popular tool among users but advisable for beginners to understand the functions of dictionary attacks.

CommonView for Wi-Fi

CommonView for Wi-Fi is Kali Linux tool, which is a network monitor for wireless networks and also used for analyzing packets. It is a simple tool, which comes with a graphical user interface that is easy to understand. The tool was developed for wireless network admins and security professionals who are interested in monitoring and troubleshooting problems related to wireless networks. The tool works with Wi-Fi 802.11 a/b/g/n/ac networks. The tool comfortably captures every packet and lets you view the network information. It also gives you other information like access points, protocol distribution, signal strength etc. The tools provides valuable information about a wireless network and comes across as a handy tool for network administrators.

Pyrit

Pyrit is also a very good Kali Linux tool which allows you to attack lets you perform attack IEEE 802.11 WPA/WPA2-PSK encrypted wireless networks. This is a freely available tool, which is hosted on Google Code. Again since it is hosted by Google, it may be taken off in the coming months and therefore, it is good to have a local copy of it. It supports a wide range of operating systems such as Linux, OS X, FreeBSD, etc.

It cracks WPS/WPA-2 passwords using the brute force attack method. Being very effective, it is suggested that everyone tries this tool out at least once.

Reporting Tools

The report you get as a result of the penetration test that you have conducted is a key deliverable in an activity carried out for security assessment. The final deliverable of penetration testing is the report, which gives a record of the service that was provided, the methods that were used, the findings or results of the tests and the recommendations that come as an output to better the security. Report making is most of the times ignored as it is found to be boring by many penetration testers. In this part, we will talk about the Kali Linux tools that are available to make the process of making reports simple. The tools help you store your penetration test results, which can be referred to when you are working on making the report. The tools will also help you communicate and share data with your team.

We are covering the 2 main tools, which are Dradis and Magic Tree.

Dradis

The Dradis framework is an open source Kali tool which functions as a platform to collaborate and report for security exports in the network security domain. The tool is developed in Ruby language and is independent of platform. Dradis provides the option to export reports and all the activities can be recorded in one single report. Exporting the report in file formats that are PDF or DOC is currently only supported in the pro version and is missing from the community version.

Magic Tree

Magic Tree is a Kali Linux tool, which is used for reporting and data management and it is much like Dradis. It is designed in a way such that data consolidation, execution of external commands, querying and generation of reports becomes an easy and straightforward process. Kali Linux has this tool pre-installed and it is located at "Reporting Tools" category. It manages the host and its associated data using the tree node structure.

Magic Tree vs. Dradis

Both Magic Tree and Dradis have been designed to solve the same set of problems i.e. data consolidation and report generation. Both Magic Tree and Dradis allow data to be imported from that which is produced by various tools used for penetration testing. It also allows data to be added manually and report generation of that data. The tree structure is followed by both the tools to store data.

Stress Testing Tools

Stress testing can be defined as a software testing methodology, which is carried out to find out the reliability and stability of a system. The test makes a system go through extreme conditions to find out how robust it can be how efficiently is can handle the errors under such circumstances.

Stress tests are designed to test systems even beyond the regular points of operation to understand how well it can handle pressure. Stress testing was introduced to ensure that a system, which is in production would not crash under extreme situations.

Let us see the various stress testing tools that are available in Kali Linux.

DHCPig

DHCPig is a Kali Linux tool that exhausts the DHCP server system by initiating an exhaustion attack on it. This tool will use up all the IPs available on the network and stop new users from being assigned any IPs, release IPs that have been already assigned to genuine devices, and then for a good amount of time, it will send out gratuitous ARP and kick all the Windows hosts from the network. The tool requires admin privileges and scapy >=2.1 library to execute. The tool does not need any configuration as such and you just have to pass the environment as a parameter on which you plan to release the test. It has been successfully tested on multiple DHCP server in Windows and on several Linux distributions.

inviteflood

Inviteflood is a Kali Linux tool, which is used to send SIP/SDP INVITE message to cause a flooding over UDP/IP.

It has been tested over several Linux platforms and it performs well on all distributions.

mdk3

MSK is a Kali Linux too which is proof-of-concept tool used to exploit the protocol weaknesses of IEEE 802.11

Note: Ensure that the network owner has permitted you to run MDK on it before you run it on the network.

FunkLoad

FunkLoad is a Kali Linux too that web tester for functions and load on a system. It is developed in Python and has the following use cases.

Testing web projects for their functionality and regression testing as well.

Test the performance of the web application by applying load on it. This helps to understand bottlenecks, and helps you to get a detailed report of the test.

Primary testing like volume testing or longevity testing would not result in showing bugs that would show up on load testing. This is achieved through FunkLoad.

It is a stress testing tool which will end up overwhelming a web application and its resources. This also helps in understanding the recoverability of the application.

You can also write scripts to automate repetitive tasks.

ipv6-toolkit

The IPV6 toolkit by SI6 Network is a set of tools to test the security of IPv6 networks and troubleshoot any problems that arise on it. You can perform real-time attacks on an IPv6 network which will help you assess the security, resiliency, and will help you troubleshoot the networking problem on IPv6 networks. The tools in this suite include tools from packet crafting tools to the most elaborate IPv6 tool out there for network scanning which is scan6 tool.

The following list will give you an idea of all the tools in the suite.

- addr6: A tool which analyzes an manipulates the IPv6 network

- flow6: And IPv6 security assessment tool

- frag6:A tool that performs fragmentation based attacks on an IPv6 network to perform a number of fragmentation related aspects and security assessment

- icmp6: A tool that performs attacks on the basis of errors thrown by ICMPv6 network protocol.

- jumbo6: A tool that looks at the handling of IPv6 jumbograms andassesses potential flaws in it.

- na6:A tool that sends arbitrary messages of neighbor advertisements.

- ni6: A tool that checks the potential flaws in processing ICMPv6 packages by sending information messages of the ICMPv6 node.

- s6: A tool that sends messages of arbitrary neighbor solicitation.

- ra6: A tool that sends messages of arbitrary router advertisements.

- rd6: A tool that sends messages of arbitrary ICMPv6 redirects.

- rs6: A tool that sends messages of arbitrary router solicitation

- scan6: A tool that scans IPv6 networks

- tcp6: A tool to send arbitrary TCP segments and perform a variety of TCP- based attacks.

SlowHTTPTest

The SlowHTTPTest is a Kali Linux tool that can simulate the Denial of Service attacks in the application layer. It is supported on most platforms such as Linx, OS X and the command line interface on Windows systems.

The tool basically implements Dos attacks of application layer which are low bandwidth in nature such as Slow HTTP POST, slowloris, Slow Read attack by leeching the concurrent pools of connection, and also the Apache Range Header attack which causes high load on the CPU and memory of a server.

The HTTP protocol due to its design, to be completely processed, requires the request to be received by the server completely. This is what the slowloris and HTTP POST denial of service attacks take advantage of. The server will reserve its resources for pending data if the HTTP request is incomplete or the rate at which the data is transferring is very slow. Thus when the server is keeping most of its resources busy, it results in the creation of denial of service. That is exactly what this tool does. It sends partial or slow HTTP requests which keeps the server busy and thus resulting in a denial of service from the target HTTP server.

Maintaining Access Tools

Once we have cracked into a target machine by using the many methods that we have looked at, our next step should be ensuring techniques that will help us maintain the precious access that we have gained. This is to make sure that if the vulnerability that let you into the system gets patched in the future, you still have some way through which you can access the system.

We will look at the various tools available in Kali Linux, which will help us to maintain access to a system.

Cryptcat Package Description

CryptCat is a simple Kali Linux utility, which reads all data that it sees across network connections and writes data to it too. It uses the UDP or TCP protocol to do this and even encrypts the data that is sent over the network. It is designed in a way such that it can be integrated in a program or a script that runs in the front-end on a graphical interface while the tool runs in the backend in a very reliable manner. At the same time, it is also a tool, which is rich in features and allows network debugging and exploration. It is a very interesting tool as it will allow you to create the connection of your choice and has many other built-in features as well.

HTTPTunnel Package Description

The HTTPTunnel is a Kali Linux tunneling software. It can create tunnels through network connections. It basically has two components.

The client side which exists behind a firewall and will accept connections on ports that are connected to a remote server or will play the role of SOCKS proxy. The authentication source for SOCKS source can be a list of fixed users which is fetched from a MySQL or LDAP directory. The client component is aPerl script that is independent of platform or is also available as a Win32 binary.

The server side component exists on the Internet to which the client makes HTTP requests. The server side then translates and forwards these requests to network connections on upstream servers, which are remote.

There are two available servers. A web server, which basically hosts a PHP script. The PHP script that you host on the web server will allow your web server to act as the server to run HTTP tunnel.

The second server is a standalone server, which runs a Perl script independent of the platform or a Win32 binary. If you have your own box like a home computer, which is connected to the Internet, it can be used as the standalone server. Hosted server may pose restrictions to the PHP script (such as maximum execution time for the PHP script which will result in limiting the time for your connections) that you are hosting on it based on the company that is providing you the hosted server. Therefore, having a standalone server of your own has an advantage over the hosted server as you have complete access to your home computer.

Intersect Package Description

Intersect 2.5 is a Kali Linux tool that is the second major release in the version that have been released so far. There is a vast difference between this release and its previous versions. This version lets the user control which features are to be included in the intersect script and has also made room for importing customized features.

The latest release mostly focuses on the ability to integrate customized intersect scripts and also on the integration of individual modules and features in the tool. The user can use the create.py application which will guide him through a user friendly process which is menu-driven and lets the user add the modules of their choice, import custom modules and create intersect scripts as per their specific requirements.

Sniffing and Spoofing Tools

When it comes to network security, Sniffing and Spoofing of packets are two very important concepts as these are two of the major threats to the security of a network. If you want to deploy security measures for a network infrastructure, understanding the treats of packet sniffing and spoofing is very important. There are many tools available on the Internet, which facilitate sniffing and spoofing such as Tcpdump, Wireshark, Netwox, etc. The tools are used extensively by both attackers and security researchers. Students should also be able to use these tools. However, it is important to understand network security to be able to learn how to make use of these tools and how packet sniffing and spoofing is used in software.

Let's go through a few tools, which are used for packet sniffing and spoofing.

Burp Suite

Burp Suite is a Kali Linux tool, which serves as a platform to run security tests on web applications. It has a number of tools that work together and make the whole testing process work seamlessly right from the initial mapping of the test and analyzing the attack surface of the application, to finding the vulnerabilities in the security and exploiting them.

Burp lets a user have full control as it allows manual techniques to be combined with automation. This helps in making the whole process effective, fast and more fun.

DNSChef

DNSChef is a highly configurable Kali Linux tool for configuring DNS proxy for Malware analysts and Penetration Testers. A DNS proxy is a fake DNS is a tool that is used for analyzing network traffic.

For example, if someone is requesting for example.com over the Internet, a DNS proxy can be used to redirect them to an incorrect page over the Internet as opposed to the real server on which the website for example.com resides.

There are a lot of tools for DNS proxy available on the Internet. Most will allow you to point the incoming DNS queries to one single IP. DNSChef was developed a complete solution for a DNS proxy tool, which would provide a user with every kind of configuration that is needed. As a result of this vision, DNSChef is a tool that works across all platforms and is capable to create fake responses while supporting multiple types of DNS records

The use of a DNS proxy is advisable in times when you cannot force a web application to use a specific proxy server. For example, there are some mobile applications, which discard proxy settings in the OS HTTP settings. In cases like these, use of a tool like DNSChecf as a DNS proxy server will come handy. It will allow you to redirect the incoming HTTP request to a desired destination by tricking the application.

Wifi Honey

Wifi Honey is a Kali Linux tool, which is essentially a script that creates five monitor interfaces. One window is used for the tool airodump-ng and the remaining four are used for APs. The tool runs the five windows in a screen session making it simple to switch between the five screens and ultimately makes this process even more comfortable. All the sessions are labelled and therefore you will not end up getting confused with the screens.

Password Attack Tools

As the name suggests, password attack tools in Kali Linux help crack passwords of applications and devices.

Let us go through a few of the password cracking devices that are available in Kali Linux.

crowbar

Crowbar, which was previously known as Levye is a Kali Linux tool which is used for penetration testing. According to authors of regular brute forcing tools, crowbar was developed to brute force protocols in a manner, which was different than the regular tools. For example, during an SSH brute force attack, most tools use the username and the password to carry the attack but crowbar unlike the majority of the tools, uses SSH keys. This means that is there was any kind of a private key that was retrieved during any of the penetration tests, it could then be used to attack servers which have SSH access.

john

John the Ripper is Kali Linux tool, which is both fast and feature-rich in its design. You can customize it to your specific needs and it also combines many other cracking methods in one simple program. There is a built-in compiler, which is a part of the C compiler, which will even allow you to define a cracking mode which is completely custom. John is available on all platforms, which means you can use the same tool everywhere you go. Additionally if you started cracking a session on one platform, you could very well continue it on another platform. Such is the portability of John.

John, out of the box, auto detects and supports the following crypt types in Unix by default.

DES based tripcodes, Windows and Kerberos/AFS hashes, OpenBSD Blowfish, FreeBSD MD5, BSDI extended DES, bigcrypt and traditional DES.

Ncrack

Ncrack is a Kali Linus tool, which is high speed and used to crack network authentication. The motive for building this tool was that corporates could check their network infrastructure and devices proactively for any flaws and loopholes such as poor passwords. Ncrack is also used by security professionals while conducting audits for their clients. A command line syntax similar to Nmap, a modular approach, and a dynamic engine that would take feedback from network and adapt its behavior, were the foundations that Ncrack was built up on. Nmap allows auditing of hosts on a large scale and that too in a reliable way.

Ncrack's list of features provide an interface that is very flexible and gives the user full control of the network operations, making it possible to perform brute force attacks that are very sophisticated in nature, providing time templates for easy usage, a runtime interaction that is much like Nmap's and many other things. Ncrack supports the protocols such as OWA, WinRM, MongoDB, Cassandra, MySQL, MSSQL, PostgreSQL, Redis, SIP, SMB, VNC, POP, IMAP, HTTP and HTTPS, Telnet, FTP, RDP and SSH

RainbowCrack

RainbowCrack is a general propose Kali Linux tool, which was an implementation of Philippe Oechslin. It is used to crack hashes, which have rainbow tables. Rainbow Crack cracks hashes of rainbow tables by making use of the time-memory tradeoff algorithm. This makes it different from hash crackers that are brute force.

A brute force hash cracker will generate all the plaintexts that are possible and then compute the hashes that correspond to the plaintext, all during runtime. It will then compare the hashes that need to be cracked with the hashes in hand. If no match is found even after comparing all available plaintexts, all results of the intermediate computation are discarded.

A time-memory tradeoff hash cracker sets up a stage for pre-computation, and all results of all hashes are stored in rainbow table. This is a time consuming computation. But on the first stage of pre-computing is over, hashes that were stored in the rainbow table can be cracked with a performance that is much better and efficient as compared to a brute force cracker.

Conclusion

I want to thank you once again for choosing this book. Kali Linux is a very advanced flavor of Linux, which is used for Security Auditing and Penetration Testing. After all the tools that we have looked at, it is pretty clear that if you want to succeed in the domain of Security Research, Kali Linux will provide with unlimited power to achieve the same. It is also clear that if you are just beginning with Linux, Kali Linux is not the place that you would want to start with as it is a highly complex operating system created and aimed at achieving one goal and that is security.

References

http://tutorialspoint.com/kali_linux/

https://docs.kali.org/

https://tools.kali.org/

44923711R00092

Printed in Poland
by Amazon Fulfillment
Poland Sp. z o.o., Wrocław